Essential Central Government

Ron Fenney

The recommended textbook for the examinations of the
National Council for the Training of Journalists

ISBN 0904677 84 2
Published by LGC Communications,
part of EMAP Business Communications,
33-39 Bowling Green Lane, London EC1R 0DA
Telephone: 0171 505 8555 Fax: 0171 278 8124
E-mail: saminav@lgc.emap.co.uk

Printed by Wednesday Press Ltd.

Contents

Preface

The National Council for the Training of Journalists Public Affairs Board devises the Council's syllabus and sets its exams. Part of the assistance which the NCTJ gives to students is to arrange for the publication of this book and its companion, *Essential Local Government*.

I was asked by LGC Communications to rewrite this book, having updated *Essential Local Government* in 1996. The changes which have happened since the third edition of this book, even over the relatively short time since its publication in 1995, prompted me to start from scratch.

I should like to acknowledge the help of two members of the NCTJ Studies Board. I am grateful to Amanda Ball of Sheffield College for letting me have a copy of Part II of the NCTJ Public Affairs Syllabus so that I at least knew what I had to write about and for reviewing my text later, when she was clearly better-informed than I was! If any errors remain, they are entirely mine. I am also grateful to Andy Martin, Deputy Editor of the *Bournemouth Evening Echo*, for some very helpful notes which I used in writing the final chapter, *'International Relations and Defence'*.

Central Government (and the European dimension which has increasing importance) is always changing. Even so, perhaps the timing of this exercise could have been better. The arrival of a New Labour government on the scene in May 1997 has made some of the subject matter covered by this book even more dynamic – and that change (some of it quite radical) will go on for some time yet.

However, I had to stop writing at some point (this was written during May/June 1997) and this text reflects the position as it was then – I hope that readers will bear that in mind and take the trouble to check that things are still the same. As a pointer, I have mentioned the possibility of further change where that seemed to be in the offing.

Ron Fenney
June 1997, Leicester

CHAPTER 1

The Constitution and the Monarchy

Basic principles of the Constitution – outline of the branches of Government – the rôle and powers of the Monarchy

The United Kingdom – a democracy

The United Kingdom consists of Great Britain (England, Wales and Scotland) and Northern Ireland. The country's proper title is the *United Kingdom of Great Britain and Northern Ireland.* The Isle of Man and the Channel Islands are not, strictly speaking, part of the UK, since they are Crown dependencies having a special relationship with the UK but having legislative, fiscal and judicial autonomy. The UK is also one of the 15 member states of the European Union.

The essential feature of a democracy is a competitive election at fairly frequent and regular intervals, in which the whole of the adult population is entitled to vote – a competition in which there is a genuine choice between at least two political parties with different ideologies and policies.

The UK is a unitary, as opposed to federal, democratic state; that is, a country where the power of government resides in a single national authority elected by its people. Given the size of the UK population (or, indeed, the population of any country), it is not really practical for the people to exercise that power directly themselves, and so it is exercised through elected representatives – a *representative democracy.* Anyone searching for an example of a representative democracy in action need look no further than the historic outcome of the UK 1997 General Election.

In addition, unlike some representative democracies which are republics, the UK also has a monarchy and can also be called a *monarchical democracy* – albeit a monarchy whose powers have been progressively reduced over the last few hundred years (as will be seen later in this Chapter).

The Constitution

Any democracy would be expected to have a *Constitution*, that is, a system of laws, customs and conventions which defines the way in which the country is to be governed and which regulates relations between the various arms of government and between the government and the individual citizen. The Constitution is particularly important in describing any limits imposed on any person or organisation exercising power of government.

Constitutions are usually to be found in a single document – such as that of the United States of America. Such documents still need to be amended later to take account of the evolution of the society to which they relate. But even then, the document itself is not the complete story – in the USA, the Supreme Court and Acts of Congress are extensively used to interpret the Constitution.

The UK's constitution is different. It is often described, wrongly, as an unwritten Constitution; in reality it is part unwritten and part written. The written part is not to be found in a single document – instead, it is derived from a variety of sources:

- *Statute* – originally made by the Sovereign, starting with Magna Carta in 1215, and more recently by various Acts of Parliament (the Parliament Acts 1911 and 1949, the Representation of the People Acts and other less obvious ones, such as the Race Relations Act 1968) and delegated legislation authorised by Parliament;

- *Common Law* – a continually evolving body of law made by judges in interpreting the royal prerogative powers of the Crown and the law and practice of Parliament;

- *Conventions* – precepts and practices which have never themselves been codified into a single document and are not directly enforceable in a court of law, but which, nonetheless, are regarded as having binding force by those who operate the Constitution (such as the privilege claimed by Parliament and the resignation of a government which loses a vote of confidence);

- *Works of authority or treatises* – works which have been written to offer guidance in clarifying uncertain areas of the Constitution, but which have persuasive, rather than binding, authority – such as Fitzherbert's *Abridgement*

8

(1516), Coke's *Institutes of the Law of England* (1628-44), Dicey's *An Introduction to the Study of the Law of the Constitution* (1885) and Erskine May's *Parliamentary Practice* (1844); and, more recently

- *European Treaties and law* – the transition of the European Community (EC) from just an economic partnership to a much closer union (EU) has brought into the constitutional equation the supranational influence of the EU institutions. For example, in a 1990 ruling (the Factortame case), the European Court of Justice *'disapplied'* UK legislation because it did not comply with EC law.

The Constitution can be amended by an Act of Parliament or by general agreement to create, vary or abolish a convention. In this way, it is said that the UK constitution can be adjusted more easily to changing political conditions and ideas.

An illustration of this is the Bill proposed in the 1997 Queen's Speech (following the New Labour victory in the General Election) for the incorporation into UK law of "the main provisions" of the European Convention on Human Rights. This should strengthen the ability of ordinary people to challenge, in the UK and EU courts, the actions of the various institutions of government.

In the same Queen's Speech, there is a proposed Bill to hold two referenda, possibly leading to a devolved Parliament in Scotland and an Assembly in Wales. These referenda would establish the true wishes of the people themselves, on the powers to be devolved, including in the case of Scotland the power to vary taxation.

This time, not only the issue itself but also the way it is being handled (the use of referenda) represent changes in the Constitution. The use of a referendum in the UK on a national basis was unknown before 1975 (whether the UK should stay in the EU) and some would argue that referenda are inconsistent, as a matter of principle, with a representative democracy. There have been referenda on only two other occasions and then on a country basis: Northern Ireland (1973 – the border with Eire) and Scotland/Wales (1979 – devolution).

The potential of the European institutions, particularly the European Court of Justice, as supranational agents for future change in the UK constitution, often without the ordinary citizen realising it, should not be underestimated.

The Rule of Law

The Rule of Law is generally accepted as one of the essential features of a free democratic society.

Defining what is meant by *the Rule of Law* is rather more difficult. One definition might be that it is the doctrine that the *arbitrary* exercise of power by, say, a government is made subordinate to well-defined and impartial principles of law. The ideas underlying this are best illustrated by quotations from some eminent commentators on constitutional issues:

One of the classic definitions was put forward in 1885 by AV Dicey in his *An Introduction to the Study of the Law of the Constitution* when he described the protection available through *ordinary* legal processes:

> *"When we say that the Supremacy or the Rule of Law is a characteristic of the English Constitution, we generally include under one expression at least three distinct though kindred conceptions. We mean, in the first place, that no man is punishable or can be made to suffer in body or goods except for a distinct breach of law established in the ordinary legal manner before the ordinary courts of the land..."*

Lord Justice Hewitt put a more modern gloss on the concept, as he believed it to be operating in the UK context, in his *The New Despotism* published in 1929:

> *"What is meant here by the 'Rule of Law' is the supremacy or dominance of law, as distinguished from mere arbitrariness, or from some alternative mode, which is not law, of determining or disposing of the rights of individuals."*

The purpose of the Rule of Law for the proper functioning of a modern society like the UK is illustrated by TD Weldon's 1953 *Vocabulary of Politics*. Although he was talking about associations, the principles also hold good for countries:

> *"Strictly speaking, there is nothing difficult or impressive about 'the Rule of Law'. It is merely a convenient way of referring to the fact that associations have rules and that unless those rules are pretty generally kept and enforced, the association breaks down and the activity which it was designed to promote becomes impracticable."*

The emphasis on the use of ordinary law and the avoidance of arbitrariness (due process of law) is one of the threads running through the Fifth Amendment to the American Constitution:

> *"... nor shall any person be subject for the same offense to be twice put in jeopardy of life and limb; nor shall be compelled in any criminal case to be a witness against himself, nor be deprived of life, liberty, or property, without due process of law."*

The rights of the individual can also be protected by the way in which the power of government is conferred on the state's institutions – especially if there is a degree of separation in the way in which that power is allocated.

In a federal state, such as the USA, the separation is achieved by splitting power between the national and state levels. Power at national level in the USA is further split between Congress and the House of Representatives, the Executive in the form of the President, and the Supreme Court.

The UK is a unitary state, so the separation is achieved at national level only.

The Separation of Powers

The various parts of government in the UK are essentially *separate*:

- *The Legislature* – which consists of the Queen in Parliament and is the supreme legislative authority.

- *The Executive*, or Government, which consists of:

  - the *Cabinet and other Ministers of the Crown*, responsible for initiating and directing national policy

  - *Government departments*, mostly under the control of Ministers, responsible for administration at national level, and

  - *public agencies* or bodies responsible for the administration of specific services and subject to Ministerial control to a varying extent;

- *The Judiciary* – which determines the *Common Law* and interprets statutes and is independent of both the Legislature and the Executive.

This arrangement, dividing the government of the country between these three elements, is often described as the *separation of powers.* Separation of powers in this way is seen as a powerful defence against concentrating too much power in the hands of a few people.

However, complete separation could lead to less efficient government, as the various elements wielded their own exclusive power without regard to the others. So, in the true spirit of British compromise, the elements often overlap, and interconnect with, one another. In this way there is a system of checks and balances to prevent excessive exercise of power by any one element.

The overlaps include, for example:

- *The Queen* is Head of the Executive and Judiciary and has a rôle in the working of the Legislature;

- *The Lord Chancellor* presides over the House of Lords part of the Legislature, manages the Judiciary on behalf of the Queen and is also part of the Executive through his membership of the Cabinet;

- *The Cabinet*, by its very nature, represents an overlap of the Executive and Legislature;

- *The House of Lords* is part of the Legislature and is also part of the Judiciary in its rôle as the ultimate domestic court of law;

- *The Judiciary*, through its judgments at the various levels of the legal process, interprets the will of the Legislature when determining the proper application of Acts of Parliament and also reviews the actions of the Executive in administrative law cases brought by individuals aggrieved at the effect of the actions of the Executive upon them.

The Sovereignty of Parliament

Parliament (which consists of the Queen, the House of Commons and the House of Lords) is the supreme legislative authority. Parliament can legislate for the UK as a whole or for one or more of its constituent countries.

Because there are no limitations imposed by an entirely written Constitution, Parliament, at least in theory, can legislate how it likes. Laws can be made, repealed or amended. Something which was unlawful before can be made lawful; something which was lawful before can be made unlawful.

Amongst other things, this ability to rewrite laws enables Parliament to reverse decisions of the Judiciary on the present state of the law which Parliament finds to be inconsistent with its real intentions. For its part, the Judiciary will always work on the assumption that there is no theoretical limit on the ability of Parliament to legislate, when interpreting Acts of Parliament in individual cases.

Conventions, which are an important part of the Constitution, can be eliminated by Parliament or can be converted into binding law, enforceable in the courts.

Parliament usually has a life of five years – but Parliament can even prolong its own life without consulting the electorate first, if Parliament believes that the circumstances justify that course of action. For that to happen, the three components of Parliament have to agree and this has only happened twice – during the two World Wars.

There are various ways in which Parliament (particularly the House of Commons) exercises control over the Executive – which can be quite effective if used skilfully by the Opposition and by the Government's own back-benchers. The mechanisms which are particularly useful include: Question time, Motions for the Adjournment of the House, Standing and Select Committees, and Motions connected with the supply of money.

The Executive is, in law, *Her Majesty's Government*, and the Ministers of the Government exercise *royal prerogative powers* on the Queen's behalf in governing the country. Ministers do not need Parliamentary authority to use these powers but if they are thought by Parliament to have abused their use, the Ministers' right to use them can be restricted or removed by Parliament.

The ultimate power of Parliament vis-à-vis the Executive is to pass a *Motion of No Confidence* or defeat the Government on an issue which the Government has identified as an *Issue of Confidence*. If this happens then, by convention, it means the end of the Government in office and, if an alternative government cannot be formed, a General Election.

The previous paragraphs together illustrate the breadth of what is known as *the Sovereignty of Parliament*, but they need to be read in a context. That context is the *political sovereignty* of the people. Parliament is itself a democratically elected body which every five years or so needs to obtain a fresh mandate from the people for whom it acts. Because of this, members of Parliament understand the importance of acting in accordance with the

Common Law and with tradition and precedent.

Although the validity of an Act of Parliament cannot be challenged in a court of law, it is probably true that Parliament would never pass legislation which commanded little or no support from the public who elected it. If, however, a Government *did* push through legislation which was not very popular, in the belief that its electoral position was very secure, it might find itself paying the price through the ballot box at the next General Election.

The political party system itself within Parliament can be argued as reinforcing Parliament's need to legislate always with one eye on the electorate – although the significance of this factor might depend upon the size of a party's majority in Parliament.

The last three paragraphs together argue for the ultimate *political sovereignty* of the people. The shape of the legislative programme in Parliament will be under the control of the political party forming the government. To arrive at that position that party would have won a General Election. The party will have set out in its election manifesto the kinds of policies it would follow, through legislation if necessary, if elected. The successful party would regard itself as having a mandate from the people for the policies in the manifesto.

Although the manifesto promises/mandate are in no sense a contract between the party/government and the people – Parliament can, and probably will, depart from the manifesto/mandate – nonetheless a series of broken promises or departures will be paid for at the next General Election. The opposition parties will also use the manifesto/mandate as a weapon against a government which is not delivering what it promised the electorate.

Finally, the context in which the sovereignty of Parliament needs to be considered is now much broader than the UK. The European Communities Act 1972 declared that European Union law would take precedence over any conflicting Act of Parliament, with the courts, ultimately the EU Court of Justice, as arbiters. In that sense, the UK's joining the EU in 1973 has not only altered the Constitution, but, some would argue, made Parliament ultimately subordinate to a supranational court, thus conceding some of its supremacy. However, it must be remembered that it was Parliament itself which conceded the point.

A Constitutional Monarchy

The Monarchy is the longest surviving secular institution in the UK; the present Queen can trace her descent directly from King Egbert who united England in 829. The only interruption to the monarchy, as an institution, was the Council of State and Oliver Cromwell from 1649 to 1660. At times, the *succession* has been interrupted and this has provided Parliament with several opportunities to increase its powers at the expense of the monarchy.

By a process of evolution, rather than revolution, over a period of a thousand years the Monarchy has changed – from one supported by the concept of the Divine Right of Kings to one which although still nominally governing the country, now does so in reality through others – a *constitutional monarchy*.

Originally, all power was exercised by the Sovereign, but not absolutely, since even then he was expected to consult the leading men of his realm, lay and clerical. Magna Carta, signed by King John in 1215, requiring the Sovereign to consult the barons, is now portrayed as a crucial constitutional document but, in fact, it would have been viewed at the time merely as a written version of the *status quo*.

The process of consultation by the Sovereign was gradually extended. The process of government itself became too complex for the Sovereign to operate himself or herself, so it had to be given to others to carry out on the Sovereign's behalf. These factors eventually resulted in the Parliamentary and Ministerial system which we see today.

Over the same period the real power was transferred from the Sovereign to Parliament so that by the beginning of the 20th century, although government was still in the Sovereign's name, political power lay elsewhere. The Sovereign could no longer control Parliament or exercise real choice of Ministers and Judges – power had finally passed to the people.

The rôles of the Sovereign

The Queen is said to 'personify the State' – the Sovereign stands for the unity of the nation and its standards as a country – she is the Head of the UK State. As a matter of strict law, she is an integral part of the Legislature, Head of the Executive, Head of the Judiciary, Commander-in-Chief of all the armed forces and the 'Supreme Governor' of the established Church of England. However, in practice, the Queen, by convention, now exercises those rôles on the advice of her Ministers.

Nonetheless, the Sovereign still has a significant rôle to play in the process of governing the UK. For example, the Queen:

- summons, prorogues and dissolves Parliament;

- gives the Royal Assent to Bills passed by Parliament;

- formally appoints Government Ministers (including the Prime Minister), judges, diplomats, governors, officers in the armed forces, and bishops and some senior Church of England clergy;

- keeps track of what the Government is doing in her name by receiving accounts of Cabinet decisions, giving audiences to Ministers (the Prime Minister is usually seen once each week), reading dispatches and signing many State papers;

- holds meetings of the Privy Council;

- issues pardons to people convicted of crime;

- exercises the royal prerogative of mercy in those Commonwealth countries which have retained that final appeal;

- confers peerages, knighthoods and other honours;

- carries out duties which although ceremonial are nonetheless important – such as the State Opening of Parliament and the Trooping of the Colour;

- entertains visiting Heads of State and undertakes formal visits to other countries;

- recognises foreign states and governments (their diplomatic representatives formally present their credentials to the Queen before they perform their duties), makes treaties and cedes or annexes territory;

- declares war and makes peace.

However, as explained earlier, most of these rôles are exercised on the advice of other people.

How the Sovereign's rôles are *really* exercised

When the Queen summons Parliament after a General Election or after prorogation, she does so at the *State Opening of Parliament* in the Palace of Westminster. This largely ceremonial but important event takes place in the chamber of the House of Lords, to which the members of the House of Commons are summoned. The *Queen's Speech*, which the Lord Chancellor hands to the Queen, sets out the programme which Her Majesty's Government will seek to implement during the next session of Parliament. The speech, *"My Government intends..."*, is not written by the Queen but is written for her by the Ministers in the Government – she has no say in its content.

The Queen can prorogue or dissolve Parliament only when formally asked to do so by the Prime Minister.

The person appointed by the Queen as Prime Minister is always the leader of the political party with the largest number of seats or able to command a working majority in the House of Commons. The other important office holders are appointed by the Queen on the advice of the Prime Minister or his/her Ministers.

The Royal Pardon is exercised only on the advice of the Home Secretary.

Honours are conferred by the Queen twice each year – on her official birthday and at New Year – and at the resignation of a Government and the dissolution of Parliament for a General Election. These honours are usually conferred on the advice of the Prime Minister. There are exceptions to this: the Order of the Garter, the Order of the Thistle, the Order of Merit and the Royal Victorian Order are the personal gift of the Queen.

A recent development has encouraged more public participation in the honours system; it is now usual for members of the public to submit the names of others whose achievements they think should be recognised through the honours system – although the final decision still rests with the Queen on the advice of the Prime Minister.

One should not, however, overlook the undoubted contribution which the Queen is in a position to make to the government of the UK.

Apart from her important rôle of symbolising the country at home and abroad, the Queen has had 45 years' experience as a constitutional monarch. During that time she has gained a wealth of knowledge about the way successive Governments have worked.

Walter Bagehot set out a classic definition of the sovereign's power in his *The English Constitution*:

> *"the right to be consulted, the right to encourage, the right to warn"*.

Although the Queen, constitutionally, has to act on the advice of her Ministers, she has been in a unique position during the weekly audiences to give advice (on a strictly non-partisan basis) to the 10 successive Prime Ministers who have come and gone. The Queen has been known to question the Prime Minister and other ministers quite closely on proposals set out in the Cabinet or Foreign Office papers which she has read. It is reputed that the Queen caught Harold Wilson out early in his premiership when, during the weekly audience, she expressed interest in a New Town proposal in the Cabinet papers – it was news to him!

Some former Prime Ministers have remarked upon the benefit they gained from the Queen's advice. Whether the individuals concerned seek that advice and how much notice they take of it, will probably depend upon their individual personality and their opinion of their own knowledge and experience.

The Queen's unique experience has also counted for much abroad – especially within the Commonwealth. The respect which the Queen commands and her calming and unifying influence have helped, it is said, to repair some of the damage caused to relations between the UK and certain Commonwealth countries by the Thatcher government on the issue of sanctions against South Africa. Some commentators even go so far as to say that without the Queen's influence, the Commonwealth could have disintegrated or the UK been expelled from it.

The Privy Council

Before the 18th Century the *Sovereign in Council* or the *Privy Council* was the main source of executive power. The Cabinet grew out of a committee of the Privy Council and as the system of Cabinet government developed with the transfer of powers to it, so the Privy Council itself became less important as an instrument of government. This explains why Ministers in the Cabinet are also Privy Councillors and meetings of the Cabinet are supposed to be 'privy' or secret. Some modern Government departments also started life as committees of the Privy Council.

These days, the principal function of the Privy Council is to advise the Queen on *Orders in Council*, including those granting royal charters of incorporation. Orders in Council are one of the types of delegated legislation *(see Chapter 2)* and their use can be quite varied – much of the delegated legislation relating to Northern Ireland is made in this way.

The Council also advises the Queen on issuing royal proclamations – some of which can be quite important, such as those summoning or dissolving Parliament.

There are now (1997) about 450 Privy Councillors and membership, usually for life, is granted by the Queen on the advice of the Prime Minister to people eminent in public, political and judicial life. Privy Councillors are also appointed from Commonwealth countries.

Although membership is for life, it can be terminated. The only time this century that a Privy Councillor has been fired was in 1921 when Sir Edgar Speyer, a philanthropist friend of Prime Minister Herbert Asquith, was convicted of collaboration with the Germans in the First World War. Since then there have been three notable resignations: John Profumo (Cabinet Minister who lied to the Commons about his relationship with Christine Keeler); John Stonehouse (former minister convicted of theft and false pretences); and Jonathan Aitken (following the collapse of his libel trial against *The Guardian* and Granada Television).

Members of the Cabinet must be Privy Councillors and, if they are not, they are granted membership of the Privy Council before they take their oath of office as members of the Cabinet. In practice, senior members of the Opposition political parties are also appointed as members of the Privy Council.

Privy Councillors are 'The Right Honourable'; so those MPs who are also Privy Councillors can be identified as such by the use of this title when they are addressed in Parliament and elsewhere. If the Privy Councillors are lawyers, their more formal title is extended to 'My Right Honourable and Learnèd Friend'.

Usually, only a small number (about four) of the Privy Councillors is invited to any meeting of the Council – which, by tradition, meets standing up (including the Sovereign), presumably helping to keep the meetings short! The only occasions when the full Privy Council is summoned are when a new Sovereign is crowned or when the existing Sovereign intends to marry.

The meetings of the Privy Council itself are largely formal. The real work of the Privy Council is done in its different kinds of committee, which the Sovereign does not attend. An example of these committees is the Judicial Committee. The Judicial Committee includes the Lord Chancellor, the Lords of Appeal in Ordinary and other Privy Councillors who hold or have held high judicial office in the UK and in the Commonwealth. The function of the Judicial Committee is to act as the final court of appeal from courts in UK dependencies, the Isle of Man, the Channel Islands and those Commonwealth countries which still recognise this method of appeal.

The administrative work of the Privy Council is done in the Privy Council Office under the supervision of the *Lord President of the Council* who is a Cabinet Minister and who, by modern convention, is also *Leader of the House of Commons*. Following the 1997 General Election this office was held, for the first time, by a woman – who wished to be known as the *President of the Council.*

How the Monarchy is funded

By 1760 George III had realised that he could no longer afford to provide for all the expenses of government from the resources then available to him. So he turned over to the Government of the time most of the Sovereign's hereditary revenues in return for an annual grant – the *Civil List.*

These days, the Queen's expenditure on her *public* duties is met from the Civil List and expenditure or grants provided by Government departments – paying for the cost of such items as the royal yacht and the aircraft of the royal squadron and the upkeep of some of the royal palaces open to the public. All of this expenditure is approved by Parliament. In 1991 the Civil List payments were frozen at £7.9 million a year for 10 years.

The Queen's *private* expenditure as *Sovereign* is met from the *Privy Purse*, mostly by revenue from the *Duchy of Lancaster*, an inheritance which since 1399 has been available to the reigning Sovereign. The Duchy is separate from the Sovereign's other possessions and is administered by the *Chancellor of the Duchy of Lancaster*, who is also a Cabinet Minister.

The Queen's *personal* expenditure as an *individual* is met from her own personal resources.

Other members of the Royal Family receive annual Parliamentary allowances under the Civil List Acts, for the performance of their public duties. However, each year the Queen refunds these allowances to Parliament apart from those for the Queen Mother and the Duke of Edinburgh.

The Prince of Wales receives nothing from the Civil List because he is entitled to receive instead the income generated by the estate of the *Duchy of Cornwall*, established by Edward III in 1337 and first made available to the Black Prince and traditionally thereafter to the Heir Apparent.

Since 1993 the Queen has paid, on a voluntary basis, income tax on her personal income and on that part of the Privy Purse used for personal purposes. She also agreed to pay tax on capital gains generated from her private investments and the private part of the assets in the Privy Purse. Inheritance tax is not paid.

Prince Charles has adopted a similar approach to paying tax on that part of the income from the Duchy of Cornwall which he uses for personal purposes.

The Commonwealth

The Commonwealth is a voluntary association of 53 states, most of which were British territories which have since become independent. The Queen is recognised as Head of the Commonwealth and is Head of State not only in Britain but also in 15 other member countries, where she is represented locally by a Governor-General appointed by her.

The Succession

As a consequence of the Act of Settlement 1700, only Protestant descendants of Princess Sophia, the Electress of Hanover (granddaughter of James I of England and James VI of Scotland) can succeed to the UK throne. This line of succession can be altered, but only if there is common agreement by the countries in the Commonwealth.

Sons of the Sovereign have precedence over daughters. If a son succeeds then he becomes King and his consort becomes Queen. If a daughter succeeds, then she becomes Queen Regnant but her husband has no special title. If the new Sovereign is a minor, then a Regency is established for the duration of the minority.

All has not gone well for the Royal Family in recent years – so much so that the Queen described 1992 as her *"Annus Horribilis"* – horrible year; due in part to the disastrous fire at Windsor Castle in November that year and the unsympathetic public response to the implications of that event for the finances of the Royal Family. There were other problems experienced by the Royal Family.

The more recent personal difficulties experienced by members of the Royal Family have led to a suggestion that consideration might be given to the implications of changing the rule of male precedence – to enable a daughter to succeed, if more appropriate. This issue may become more prominent in the next few years.

CHAPTER 2

The Legislature

The composition, powers and rôle of the Legislature – the process of making legislation – the conduct of the affairs of Parliament

Parliament

As explained earlier, Parliament consists of three elements – the Sovereign, the House of Commons and the House of Lords; each is separate and constituted on different principles. The chambers in which the two Houses meet are located in the *Palace of Westminster*, which is usually referred to as the *Houses of Parliament*. The three elements meet formally in the same place only on one occasion, the State Opening of Parliament.

There are two Houses of Parliament for historical reasons. The Sovereign was expected to meet all the normal expenses of government from his own resources. If more was needed, for special purposes such as fighting a war, the Sovereign had to go cap in hand to the barons and clergy (the Great Council – the forerunner of the House of Lords) for the extra money. This started in the 13th century.

After a period, even this combined source was not enough, so in the 14th century the Sovereign began to call as well upon the representatives of counties, cities and towns for help (the community representatives or commons – the forerunner to the House of Commons).

These two groups, with the Sovereign, were collectively called 'Parliament', that is a meeting for the purpose of discussion or parley. At various times during the 14th century the two groups met in separate places and from this developed the two chambers of Parliament, the House of Lords and the House of Commons.

As time went on, the Commons came to realise the strength of their position. In the 14th century the Sovereign accepted that taxes should not be levied without the assent of Parliament. During the 15th century the Commons obtained the right to take an active part in converting into law their requests – their 'Bills'.

The position of the Commons was secured in the Glorious Revolution of 1688, when James II fled and the throne was offered by Parliament to William and Mary on condition that henceforth the Sovereign could not legislate or suspend laws without the assent of Parliament.

Parliament still looked to the Executive – originally the Sovereign and later the Sovereign's Ministers in Cabinet – to initiate changes in policy. The Reform Act 1832, by extending the electorate by 49% and abolishing the Rotten Boroughs, started a process of change which steadily reduced what then remained of the Sovereign's influence on the Commons.

Even today, the House of Commons jealously guards its independence from the Sovereign – best illustrated by the ceremonial slamming of the doors of the House of Commons in the face of Black Rod when he comes from the House of Lords to summon the Commons to attend the Queen in the House of Lords, for the State Opening of Parliament.

The functions of Parliament

The powers of Parliament have been described in the section in Chapter 1 which discusses the Sovereignty of Parliament. The section in the same chapter on the Separation of Powers makes the point that Parliament is not, and never has been, part of the Executive – the Sovereign's Ministers.

Although the phrase 'Parliamentary government' is sometimes used to describe the UK's form of government, this can give a misleading impression. The phrase should be read to mean government *through* Parliament, rather than government *by* Parliament. Public policy is formulated by the Executive and put before Parliament for discussion and approval or rejection. The initiative usually lies with the Executive, not Parliament – which is essentially reactive in the business of government.

The functions of Parliament are:

● to make laws;

● to enable Government to function by voting for the
   taxation needed to fund it;

- to examine Government policy and the way it is administered; and

- to provide a forum where major issues of the day can be debated.

The House of Commons

As a result of recent boundary changes introduced on the recommendation of the *Parliamentary Boundary Commissions* for the 1997 General Election, the House of Commons is now composed of a total of 659 MPs:

England	529
Scotland	72
Wales	40
Northern Ireland	18

The result of the 1997 General Election was generally regarded by most commentators as historic, given, amongst other things, the size of the Labour Party majority (330 seats were needed for an overall majority):

Labour	419
Conservative	165
Liberal Democrat	46
Ulster Unionist Party	8
Scottish National Party	6
Plaid Cymru	4
Democratic Unionist Party	4
Social Democrat and Labour Party	3
Sinn Fein	2
United Kingdom Unionist Party	1
Independent	1

Why can that result be fairly described as 'historic'? Perhaps it is because:

- the Labour Party achieved its largest number of seats since its foundation as a political party at the beginning of this century;

- the Liberal Democrats doubled their number of seats, giving them the largest number of seats held by any third party since 1929;

- the Conservative Party's share of the vote (31.4%) was its lowest since 1832, when modern elections were introduced by the Reform Act of that year;

- the Conservative Party was wiped out in the larger English cities and in Scotland (for the first time) and in Wales (last time was 1906) – raising interesting questions about which party could now claim to be the official Opposition in those countries;

- the number of women MPs was increased from 62 to 119, the largest ever – of whom 101 were Labour, possibly due in part to the all-women shortlist approach adopted by Labour for a brief period in some parts of the country;

- the number of MPs from ethnic minorities was the largest ever and, later, the first black Minister was appointed; and

- the first ever truly independent MP was elected for the Tatton constituency – Martin Bell, *"the man in the white suit"*.

The House of Lords

The House of Lords consists of the Lords Spiritual and the Lords Temporal, none of whom is elected – a source of some debate, which is dealt with later in this chapter.

The *Lords Spiritual* are:

- the Archbishops of Canterbury and York;

- the Bishops of London, Durham and Winchester; and

- the 21 next most senior diocesan bishops of the Church of England.

The *Lords Temporal* are:

- all hereditary peers of England, Scotland, Great Britain and the United Kingdom (but not Ireland);

- Lords of Appeal or 'law lords' – life peers (not all of whom are still active) created to help the House in its judicial rôle as final court of appeal in the UK; and

- all other life peers created under the Life Peerages Act 1958.

Hereditary peers can sit in the House of Lords, provided they are over 21 and have proved their claim to the title.

It is possible for a peer to disclaim a peerage for his or her lifetime (but it can be reversed), without affecting the rights of their successors. This can be done by people who prefer to make their contribution to public life in the House of Commons. Examples are Tony Benn (formerly Lord Stansgate), Sir Alec Douglas-Home (Lord Home) and Quintin Hogg (Lord Hailsham). Sir Alec Douglas-Home became Prime Minister – an office which is now only held by a member of the House of Commons; and Quintin Hogg changed his mind later after a period in the Commons and became Lord Hailsham again, to be appointed as Lord Chancellor, presiding over the House of Lords.

Peers can also apply for leave of absence for the duration of a Parliament, if they do not wish to attend; about 70 had obtained this leave during the last Parliament.

Peerages of both kinds, hereditary and life, are created by the Sovereign on the advice of the Prime Minister – usually to recognise service in politics or public life or because one of the political parties has decided to put the individual in the House of Lords.

In terms of numbers (as at April 1996) there was a total of 1,197 members in the House of Lords. The number of life peers increases steadily as a consequence of the Honours lists. The 26 Lords Spiritual were joined by 1,171 Lords Temporal (767 hereditary peers and 404 life peers, of whom 24 were law lords). In reality, the average daily attendance is about 360.

Unlike their counterparts in the House of Commons, members of the House of Lords receive no salary, but they can claim expenses, within statutory limits.

The Lord Chancellor presides over meetings of the House of Lords as ex-officio Speaker, sitting on the *Woolsack* – a large cushion-shaped seat stuffed with wool from several Commonwealth countries, a tradition which has its origins in the Middle Ages when wool was the main source of the country's wealth.

However, the Lords must be expected to be a calmer place than the Commons – the words *"Order! Order!..."* will never be heard in the Lords, because it is the House itself, rather than its Speaker, which is responsible for keeping order in its debates!

The meeting of Parliament

The life of a Parliament is up to five years, divided into *sessions*, each normally lasting about a year – usually beginning and ending in October/ November.

Each session begins with the State Opening of Parliament, with the Queen's Speech outlining the Government's legislative plans for that session. A session comes to an end by Parliament being *prorogued* and is said to 'stand prorogued' until the next session begins, usually after about a week. Public Bills which have not been passed by the time Parliament is prorogued are lost – so there tends to be an acceleration of the legislative process towards the end of a session after the summer recess.

The sessions are *adjourned*: on each sitting day; over the weekend; for recesses at Christmas, Easter and the Spring Bank Holiday; and for a long summer recess starting in late July.

The average annual number of sitting days is about 159 for the Commons and 140 for the Lords.

Both Houses of Parliament hold their meetings in public and their deliberations are now accessible to many more people since they are covered by radio and television. As far as the Commons is concerned, the Speaker's cry: *"Order! Order!..."* should now be well known!

The minutes and speeches in the Houses are transcribed verbatim and published daily in *Hansard* – now published by HMSO, but originally (1774-1892) compiled and printed by Messrs Hansard.

The records of the Lords from 1497 and the Commons from 1547 are available to the public through the House of Lords Record Office.

Parliamentary Privilege

Each House of Parliament has rights, privileges and immunities to protect it from unwarranted interference in carrying on its work – these are enjoyed by each House collectively and by each member individually.

These rights include freedom of speech (actions for defamation cannot be brought for what is said in Parliament); freedom from arrest in civil actions; exemption from serving on a jury; the collective right of access to the Monarch; the right of each House to control its own proceedings (including excluding the public, 'strangers', if it wishes) and to punish any person for breach of any of its privileges or for contempt.

Members of Parliament

Members of Parliament are elected to the House of Commons through universal suffrage – all people over the age of 18 and eligible to vote having a say in who should be their representative. The ballot is secret and unlike some countries, such as Australia, voting is not compulsory.

Once elected, an MP has responsibilities to his or her constituents and to his or her party, both locally and at Westminster.

An MP is expected to represent the interests of all his or her *constituents* regardless of how they voted. Any constituent who feels aggrieved about an issue will almost certainly write to their MP to enlist his or her help in trying to resolve the problem – the MP will then write to the relevant Minister, Government department or local authority, intervening on the constituent's behalf. MPs receive an allowance to help them deal with this correspondence, often enabling them to employ a secretary or researcher. Space is so limited at Westminster that not every MP can be given office space, even on a shared basis.

As far as the *party* is concerned, most MPs will have been adopted as the official candidate of a political party, through a formal selection process. As a result of that they will receive financial and other practical support for fighting their election campaign – from their party at national and local level and from organisations having some sort of affinity with the aims of their party (for example, many Labour MPs are sponsored by a trade union).

MPs will spend a large part of their time at Westminster, but, if they are sensible, they will return to their *constituencies* quite frequently to meet the officers of their local party or association to keep them informed and to meet, face-to-face, with their constituents at advertised *'surgeries'* in the constituency. Keeping the local party or association informed is important, even if the seat is a safe one, because there is always the risk of deselection – even local Conservatives are prepared to ditch a sitting MP if he or she is believed to have become an electoral liability.

As far as *Westminster* is concerned, MPs will have campaigned on some local issues but largely on the basis of the policies set out in their party's election manifesto. Consequently, when the time comes to implement that manifesto, the MPs will be expected by their party hierarchy to vote according to their party line on any issues coming before the House of Commons.

Occasionally, if the issue is recognised as one which should be decided according to individual conscience (for example, the reintroduction of capital punishment), the MPs will be allowed to vote as they wish – a 'free vote'. Adherence to the party line – party discipline – is maintained through the whip system.

As a matter of last resort, an MP whose political behaviour displeases the

Chief Whip can have the 'whip withdrawn' from them, usually until they see the error of their ways – this excludes them from the party's meetings and information systems within the House, but they still remain MPs. A recent example of this was the withdrawal of the whip from a group of Eurosceptic Conservative MPs for a time in the final year of the last Parliament.

Whips and votes in Parliament

Government business is steered through Parliament by the *Government Chief Whip* in each House, under the direction of the Prime Minister and the Leaders of the two Houses, and in consultation with the *Opposition Chief Whip*.

The Leader of the House of Commons is a Minister of the Crown and a member of the Cabinet, now usually also holding the office of *[Lord] President of the Council*. The Leader has prime responsibility for organising the business of the House and responding to the wishes of the House for opportunities to debate matters of concern to it.

The Government Chief Whip in the House of Commons is formally known as the *Parliamentary Secretary to the Treasury*. The Government Chief Whip has a Deputy and a number of Assistants to help him or her. Their job is to implement the decisions of the Leader of the House.

Sometimes the phrases *'usual channels'* or *'behind the Speaker's Chair'* are used in Parliament, particularly when an issue has arisen and someone has to find time for it in the programme of business. This phrase refers to the Whips as a group who meet to reach agreement on the changes to the programme needed to accommodate the new issue.

The Whips keep their respective members informed of forthcoming parliamentary business through issuing the *Weekly Whip* – often with the aim of ensuring that their voting strength is maintained. If an issue is especially important to their party, the item will be underlined three times in the list from the Whip – *a three-line whip* – and the MP or Peer will be expected to attend to vote, with no excuses (even illness) being accepted!

However, individual MPs can avoid having to attend to vote and yet maintain their party's voting strength by *pairing* with an Opposition MP – both agreeing not to vote and, in effect, cancelling each other's votes. These arrangements, which have to be approved by the Whips, are frequently used by MPs who would find it difficult to attend to vote.

The pairing system is a sensible and convenient one, but it is based on custom and practice and can be unilaterally withdrawn by any party at any time. This was done by the Labour Party in the last few months prior to the 1997 General Election, because of perceived abuse of the pairing system by the Conservatives – with the consequence that MPs on both sides, some of whom were quite ill, had to make the journey to Westminster to vote, especially since the Government's majority was by then in single figures.

Often the Speaker first tries to declare the result of a vote on the basis of the volume of support for or against the proposition when it is put to the vote. If that approach is challenged, the Speaker orders the lobbies to be cleared and a *Division* is held. The Division Bells ring throughout the Palace of Westminster and in certain premises in the neighbourhood, where MPs may usually be found.

It is then a race against time (usually about eight minutes) for any MP hearing the bells to get (often running on foot!) to the relevant lobby alongside the chamber – *Ayes* (to the right of the Speaker) or *Noes* (to the left) – and have his or her vote recorded by the tellers (two in each lobby), before the doors are closed. After the votes are counted, the four tellers hand the result to the Speaker who announces the result formally to the House.

Front, Back and Cross Benches

In the House of Commons there are two rows of benches down either side of the chamber. The Speaker sits at one end, between the two rows of benches, behind a large table on which, amongst other things, sits the Mace (which is a symbol of power) and two despatch boxes.

The members of Her Majesty's Government, by tradition, sit on the *front bench* on the Speaker's right hand. The members of the Official Opposition (in effect the shadow cabinet) sit on the opposite *front bench*. Any person speaking on behalf of the Government or the Opposition will rise and go to the despatch box to speak.

MPs who are not members of the Government or the Opposition will sit on the other benches on the relevant side of the chamber – the *back benches*. Such MPs are known as back bench MPs and the way in which they can participate in the business of the House is dealt with later.

Much the same arrangement is adopted in the House of Lords (where, incidentally, the seats are red, rather than green!), but with some important differences. The meetings there are presided over by the Lord Chancellor sitting on the Woolsack and there is an extra set of benches, directly facing the Lord Chancellor, for those peers (Bishops, Law Lords and others) who do not espouse any political party – the *cross benches*.

MPs never resign!

MPs usually hold office until the dissolution of Parliament just before the next General Election. A casual vacancy can be caused by death, elevation to the House of Lords or by 'resignation'. Strictly speaking, an MP cannot resign in the ordinary sense of the word and if that is the result they wish to achieve, then they must disqualify themselves by applying to the Chancellor of The Exchequer for appointment either as *Steward or Bailiff of the Chiltern Hundreds* or *Steward of the Manor of Northstead*. These are recognised technically as offices of profit under the Crown, even though they are unpaid, and lead to automatic disqualification from holding office as an MP.

The two main political parties in Parliament

Although the Liberal Democrats would like to think otherwise, there is a predominantly two party system in the UK – it has been so for the past 150 years. Since 1945 those two parties have been the Conservative and Labour parties. The Conservative and Labour parties organise themselves differently in Parliament.

The Conservative and Unionist Members' Committee (the 1922 Committee) consists of all Conservative back bench MPs in the Commons. The basis upon which the Conservative front bench can attend meetings of the 1922 Committee depends upon whether the party forms the Government or the Opposition. If there is a Conservative Government, then Ministers can attend meetings of the 1922 Committee only by invitation; if in Opposition, all Conservative MPs, including those in the shadow cabinet, have the right to attend.

The Parliamentary Labour Party consists of all members of the party in both the House of Commons and the House of Lords. Again, how matters are arranged depends upon whether there is a Labour Government. If there is a Labour Government, then communications between the Government and its back benchers in both Houses are handled by a parliamentary committee – half are elected by the back benchers themselves and half are representatives appointed by the Government. If the party is in Opposition, the affairs of the Parliamentary Labour Party are organised by a parliamentary committee – this time entirely elected – which also acts as the Labour shadow cabinet.

The organisation of these parties, and the Liberal Democrat Party, outside Parliament is described in a later chapter.

The Speaker

The Speaker is the most important officer of the House of Commons – and is often regarded as the First Commoner in the Land. The office of Speaker is held by a serving MP who is not a minister of the Crown, chosen, as the first item of business in each session, by all the other MPs and holds office until retirement.

One of the rôles of the Speaker is, literally, to speak for the Commons in its dealings with the Sovereign and the Lords. When first taking office, the Speaker sometimes appears to be reluctant and needs to be dragged to the chair by his or her sponsors – this is one of the many odd customs of the House of Commons and may be due to natural modesty; but it may have something to do with the fact that in previous centuries the job of Speaker could be risky if the Sovereign was not favourably disposed towards the Commons!

The Commons' choice of Speaker has then to be approved by the Sovereign and this is done in a formal ceremony in the House of Lords, before the Lord Chancellor and the Lords Commissioners. The Commons' choice is always approved and the Speaker goes on, in the name and on behalf of the Commons of the United Kingdom, to claim:

> *"their ancient and undoubted rights and privileges, and*
> *especially to freedom from arrest, to freedom of speech in*
> *debate, and to free access to Her Majesty whenever*
> *occasion may require it, and to the most favourable*
> *construction of all their proceedings."*

which he or she always receives.

On taking office the Speaker discards any previous party allegiance. The Speaker and the three Deputy Speakers do not normally vote and do not speak except to fulfil their office. If there is a tied vote, the Speaker has to cast a vote, one way or the other, to break the deadlock but will not comment on the merits of the issue; the vote will usually be cast in favour of the government, as a matter of convention.

The Speaker lives in an apartment in the Palace of Westminster (Speaker's House) and will spend most of his or her working life in the Palace. The apolitical nature of the Speaker's office means that special arrangements are made, by tradition, to protect the interests of the Speaker as a sitting MP and the interests of the Speaker's own constituents. Being Speaker is a full-time job, so the normal constituency work of an MP is undertaken for the Speaker by MPs in adjoining constituencies. When the time comes for the Speaker to seek re-election as an MP at a General Election, the other main parties will not, by tradition, field candidates to oppose the Speaker.

The Speaker's most public rôle is presiding over meetings in the House, trying to maintain order and apply the standing orders of the House in sometimes heated debates. MPs wishing to contribute to a debate must rise in their seat and wait until called upon by the Speaker. Generally speaking, an MP can speak only once on an issue, unless the House has decided to sit 'in committee' – when the rules of debate are more relaxed.

Parliamentary procedure is based on custom and precedent, which are only partly covered by its Standing Orders. The Speaker has to enforce the rules of the House, ensuring that the proper procedure is followed and minority rights protected. If a particular point of difficulty is not covered by the Standing Orders, the Speaker will then have to fall back on previous practice to find the answer and will often consult and quote from a famous treatise on Parliamentary procedure, *Parliamentary Practice*, originally written by *Erskine May* in 1844, but regularly updated since.

Sometimes, even custom and precedent fails the Speaker, as happened in May 1997 when the two Sinn Fein MPs Martin McGuinness and Gerry Adams were not permitted the normal facilities enjoyed by MPs in Parliament because they refused to swear the MPs oath of allegiance to the Crown. The circumstances were unprecedented but that did not prevent the Speaker, Betty Boothroyd, from making a decision which she thought to be right and which would be supported by most, if not all, of the other MPs.

The powers of the Speaker are considerable:

- controlling the debates, including deciding when the debate on an issue should end and be voted upon and adjourning or suspending a sitting if matters get out of hand;

- certifying some Bills as *'Money Bills'*, which affects the way they are handled and effectively prevents the House of Lords from delaying their passage;

- ordering an MP who has broken the rules to leave the chamber or starting the process of suspending an MP for a period;

- signing various warrants, including committal to prison for contempt of the House;

- administering the House through chairmanship of the House of Commons Commission; and

- notionally chairing the Boundary Commissions.

Parliamentary Committees

There are four kinds of parliamentary committee: Committee of the Whole House, Standing Committee, Select Committee and Joint Committee.

Either House can turn itself into a *Committee of the Whole House* to debate Bills in detail after their Second Reading – the Committee Stage. This arrangement enables unrestricted discussion, by the House itself, suspending the usual rule of only one speech per member. The very important Bills, having constitutional implications or which are emergency measures, are dealt with in this way.

House of Commons *Standing Committees* are set up to consider Public Bills, clause by clause, at the Committee Stage and then report their findings to the House. Standing Committees do not have names, but are referred to by letters of the alphabet – Standing Committee A etc. A new committee is set up for each Bill, of between 16 and 50 MPs, reflecting the political balance in the House. There are Scottish, Welsh and Northern Ireland Grand Committees to consider the principles of Bills specifically relating to those countries. There are also standing committees to discuss proposed European legislation and to examine statutory instruments made by the Government. The House of Lords has a similar kind of arrangement, although the standing committees there are differently named and constituted.

Select Committees are set up by the House of Commons for a specific job, usually involving some sort of investigation and scrutiny or to deal with 'housekeeping' issues. The system of select committees was last reviewed in 1979. A select committee can be established for a Parliament, for a session, or for as long as necessary. There is a range of Select Committees which are more or less permanent and spend their time examining the work of specific Government departments and related agencies and they can build up an expertise on the particular Government department they cover. Such select committees are powerful and can require Ministers, civil servants and, indeed, any person or body, to attend for questioning. The results of these investigations by the select committees are an important check on the Executive, can be debated in the House and are published. There are fewer select committees in the House of Lords (because scrutiny of the Executive is not practised there), covering the judicial activities of the House, the European Community and Science and Technology.

Joint Committees, having members drawn from both Houses, are appointed for each session to deal with *Consolidation Bills* (a Consolidation Bill is one which does not involve new law, but merely brings together existing statutes to simplify matters – and therefore is taken through an expedited procedure because detailed scrutiny is not required) and to deal with delegated legislation.
Back benchers

The back benchers have an important rôle in checking on the intentions and actions of the Executive and are able to do so in a variety of ways. Although what follows relates to the House of Commons, broadly similar opportunities exist for back bench members of the House of Lords.

One of the most serious Parliamentary 'crimes' which can be committed by a Minister is deliberately 'misleading' the House when explaining his or her actions to the House – this is usually regarded as sufficient to mean that the Minister should do the decent thing and resign as a Minister.

The term 'mislead' is used because, by custom, the word 'lie' cannot be used by one MP of another in the Commons. The most topical example can be found in the speech made by former Home Office Minister Ann Widdicombe about the former Home Secretary Michael Howard, in the Commons in May 1997, during the law and order debate on the Queen's Speech. This was an attempt to stymie his chances of winning the Tory Party leadership after John Major lost the 1997 General Election. She described Michael Howard as having "an exquisite way with words" and she accused him of misleading the House by "denial and refuge in semantic prestidigitation" in giving his version of the circumstances surrounding the dismissal of the Governor of Parkhurst Prison after the mass breakout of IRA prisoners from there.

Questions can be raised in a variety of ways; the questions (of whatever kind) and their answers are recorded in *Hansard*.

Question Time lasts for 55 minutes on Monday, Tuesday, Wednesday and Thursday, during which Government Ministers answer MPs questions of which they have been given prior notice.

There is a separate *Prime Minister's Question Time* during which the Prime Minister answers questions (PMQs). Until recently, those questions were fairly bland, asking the Prime Minister about his diary commitments in the forthcoming week – the sting was always in the supplementary question of which the Prime Minister had often had no prior notice.

PMQs have now changed. The time allowed used to be 15 minutes on Tuesday and Thursday, but is now 30 minutes on Wednesday. The reason given by Tony Blair for this change was that he believed that answers to PMQs under John Major had become increasingly argumentative, superficial and largely a waste of time. It remains to be seen whether the new arrangement is any better at producing a more worthwhile exercise in holding the Prime Minister to account.

Finally, MPs can also put questions to Ministers for a *written answer* –

these tend to deal with specific detailed issues. There are about 50,000 of these each year.

Questions of whatever kind are just answered – there is no immediate debate on their subject matter – but one might be promised for later.

Adjournment Debates are a useful tool for MPs to raise, for debate, issues of concern to their constituents. There are three types. Just before the House adjourns for the night at the end of each business day there is a 30-minute period in which such issues can be raised and debated. A similar, but longer (three hours), opportunity exists before the House adjourns for each recess.

Finally, at the end of Question Time, MPs can seek to move the adjournment of the House, in order to provide an opportunity to debate a *"specific and important matter that should have urgent consideration"*. This rarely succeeds, but when it does the issue is debated for three hours, usually on the following day, in an *Emergency Debate*.

As an experiment to do with changing the working hours of Parliament, opportunities now exist for an adjournment debate on some Wednesday mornings – whether this will become a permanent feature remains to be seen.

Issues can also be raised in a way which provides MPs with a means of gauging the support of other MPs for their concerns. Each day, *Early Day Motions* can be tabled for debate; they are seldom debated but their real purpose is the number of other MPs who have signed them in support. The amount of this support can be of real help to an MP seeking to persuade the Government to address the concerns in other ways.

There are 20 *Opposition Days* in each session, when the Opposition is able to choose the subject for debate. The 20 days are shared – 17 are used by the Leader of the Opposition and three by the Leader of the third largest party.

Back bench MPs can also use the opportunities for debate provided by the Queen's Speech, by any motions for the *censure of the Government* (which come out of the Government's time), and during the consideration of legislation.

Membership of Standing and Select Committees provides back bench MPs with the opportunity to put the Executive to the test.

Individual MPs can also gain the opportunity to introduce their own Bills into Parliament, although their chances of success in having their proposals turned into law are not very great.

Types of legislation

There two main types of legislation – primary legislation and secondary (or subordinate or delegated) legislation. *Primary legislation* comprises the Bills passed by Parliament. *Secondary legislation* comprises Orders in Council, Statutory Instruments and local bylaws.

The trend over the last 20 years has been for the principles, only, of the more complex legislation to be covered by primary legislation (Enabling Acts), with the detail being filled in later (occasionally, never) by statutory instrument. Often, at the time of the passage of the Enabling Act, the Government does not yet know how the principles enshrined in the Act will be translated into detail later through statutory instruments.

White and Green Papers

The Government can consult people and bodies on its legislation through White and Green Papers – but does not always do so. Where the Government has a clear idea of what it wants to do and how that is to be done, it can issue a *White Paper* for consultation, inviting comments on the detail of its proposals. The White Paper itself can be debated in Parliament.

However, the Government's thinking on an issue may not yet have crystallised and it can invite more fundamental comments on how the issue might be dealt with – through a *Green Paper*.

Primary legislation

There are four types of primary legislation: Public Bills, Private Members' Bills, Private Bills and Hybrid Bills.

A *Public Bill* is one introduced by the Government to alter the general law of the land, usually to give effect to the proposals set out in the Queen's Speech. Such Bills are intended to be of general application throughout the UK or in any of its constituent countries. They can be introduced either in the House of Commons or in the House of Lords.

A *Private Members' Bill* can arise in one of two ways. Early in each session, MPs can take part in a ballot for the opportunity to introduce a Bill on one of 20 Fridays in the session where Private Members' Bills take precedence over Government business – the first 20 names drawn in the ballot are the winners. The second method involves the use of *'the 10 minute rule'*. On most Tuesdays and Wednesdays, for a short period at the beginning of public business, individual MPs can seek leave to introduce their Bill – if the motion is opposed, the MP can make a short speech for 10 minutes in support and the opposing member a short speech against.

Private Members' Bills which involve the expenditure of public money cannot go to the committee stage unless the Government agrees to finance the Bill's proposals. Private Members' Bills seldom make much progress, but some do – for example: the Marriage Act 1994 and the Building Societies (Joint Account Holders) Act 1995. Quite often Private Members' Bills gain the support of the Government and are then effectively taken over by it.

A *Private Bill* is one which is promoted by local authorities or other bodies or individuals to extend their powers or to authorise them to carry out local projects such as railways, roads and harbours, often affecting the rights of specific individuals. The Proposers of these Bills have to follow a stringent special process to persuade Parliament to give them powers which go beyond, or are in conflict with, the general law. This involves the Proposers having to give evidence and answer questions from the Parliamentary committee and from any objectors – and the objectors themselves can appear and put their case.

A *Hybrid Bill* is one which is introduced as a Public Bill but which is found to affect private interests. Such a Bill follows a special procedure which uses parts of the Public and Private Bills processes, giving the private interests affected by the Bill a chance to put their case.

Subordinate Legislation

Secondary, Subordinate, or Delegated, legislation can be made by a Minister of the Crown or by statutory corporations or local authorities, provided they follow the specific procedure laid down by Parliament when it delegated the power to legislate. There are three main groups: Orders in Council, Statutory Instruments, and local bylaws.

Orders in Council are submitted by Ministers for approval by the Sovereign at a meeting of the Privy Council. Parliament usually, but not always, agrees the draft Order in Council before it is submitted by the Minister. Much of the delegated legislation relating to Northern Ireland is made in this way.

Statutory Instruments are made by Ministers (often to flesh out the detail in a new Enabling Act or update the detail in an old one) but require the agreement of Parliament. The Enabling Act will usually specify which procedure is to be followed – affirmative or negative – in seeking Parliament's agreement.

The *affirmative procedure* means that the Statutory Instrument will not come into existence unless positively approved by resolution of Parliament. The *negative procedure* means that the Statutory Instrument will come into effect automatically if, after 40 days, no resolution has been passed objecting to it.

Most statutory instruments (there are about 2,000 each year) are scrutinised by the Select Committee on Statutory Instruments, rather than by the main body of MPs.

Local Authority *Bylaws* require the approval of a Minister but are not, themselves, considered by Parliament itself.

The stages of a Bill

A Bill can start in the House of Commons or the House of Lords. A simplified description of the process which a Bill follows in the House of Commons is:

- *First Reading:* when the Bill is first presented, there is no debate and only its title (not its contents) is read out. The Bill will be printed (but not Private Members' Bills) and will then await its Second Reading, which may be on the next day or several weeks later;

- *Second Reading:* this is the first time that the proposals in the Bill are debated and voted on – but just the general principles at this stage. If the Bill obtains its Second Reading it goes on to its Committee Stage;

- *Committee Stage:* the Bill is usually referred to a standing committee for detailed consideration and amendment, clause by clause. However, the Committee Stage can be carried out by the House itself – a Committee of the Whole House. This happens where the Bill needs to be passed urgently or where the Bill contains proposals of significance for the Constitution. In some cases, a combination of a standing committee and a Committee of the Whole House is used – this process is nearly always used for the annual Finance Bill;

- *Report Stage:* the results of the Committee Stage are reported on the floor of the House and further amendments can be made before the Bill goes on to its Third Reading, which is usually straight away;

- *Third Reading:* at this point the Bill is reviewed and debated in its final form – in the Commons detailed amendment is not allowed, but in the Lords the Bill can be amended even at this stage. Once a Bill has been read a third time, it is passed to the House of Lords;

- *The House of Lords:* always referred to as *'another place'*. The Bill goes through much the same process again, but the Committee Stage in the House of Lords is usually taken on the floor of the House – a Committee of the Whole House;

- *Lords Report to the Commons:* amendments made by the second House must be agreed by the first House before the Bill can receive the Royal Assent. If there are significant differences, then a Joint Committee is set up to try to resolve them. If agreement cannot be reached on a Bill which started in the Lords, it is unlikely to become law, because no time will be allocated for its further debate in the Commons. Under the Parliament Acts, the Lords cannot delay a money Bill started in the Commons and can only delay any other kind of Commons Bill by up to 13 months – after which time the Bill is presented to the Sovereign for the Royal Assent, regardless of the views of the Lords;

- *Royal Assent:* this is given (not personally since 1854) by the Sovereign in Norman French, *'La Reine le Veult'*, and has not been refused since 1707. The Bill is now an Act and part of the law of the land, as reflected in the sentence which precedes every Act:

  "Be it enacted by the Queen's Most Excellent Majesty, by and with the advice and consent of the Lords Spiritual and Temporal, and Commons, in this Parliament assembled, and by authority of the same, as follows:-"

Speeding up the process

The passage of a Bill through its various stages can be delayed, deliberately, by excessively long speeches by the Opposition or the submission of hundreds of amendments – with the aim of preventing it ever reaching the end of the legislative process and becoming law.

This can be prevented by the Government having Parliament pass a *timetable motion*, usually referred to as a *'guillotine'*, which limits the time to be taken by the various stages of the Bill. This guarantees that the Bill will be passed by any deadline which the Government may have in mind and tends to concentrate the Opposition's mind on what clauses in the Bill are really important!

The guillotine was first used in 1887 on the Criminal Law Amendment (Ireland) Bill following a marathon debate in the Commons lasting some 35 days – and some all-night sittings. The most recent example of such a motion was that in June 1997 for the Referendums [sic] (Scotland and Wales) Bill, when 250 amendments had been put down for debate, threatening to stall the whole devolution process. Although some Conservatives described New Labour's actions as "the most drastic way of silencing debate known to Parliament" – "Stalinist Dictatorship" – their own government had regularly used the device – a record 10 times in the 1988/89 session.

Another way of bringing a debate to a conclusion, so that a vote can be taken before the Bill is talked out, is a *Motion of Closure*. This, however, requires a petition to be submitted to the Speaker by not less than 100 MPs. Even if 100 sympathetic MPs sign up to the petition, the final decision still rests with the Speaker.

If there are many amendments to a Bill which are substantially similar, then these can be grouped together by the Speaker and the House business managers, so that they are effectively debated as a group and only once – thus saving Parliamentary time. This process is sometimes referred to as a *Kangaroo*.

The Opposition

In any healthy democracy, the Opposition has an important rôle to play. In the UK, the Opposition is regarded as the party having the highest number of seats in the Commons after the party which has formed the Government. The Opposition party is known as *Her Majesty's Loyal Opposition*.

This recognition is taken one stage further by the Leader of the Opposition, the Opposition Chief Whip and the Opposition Deputy Chief Whip receiving additional allowances to enable them to carry out their responsibilities in Opposition.

The Opposition can contribute positively to the legislative process by proposing amendments to Bills – amendments which, although they might reflect Opposition policies, are nevertheless an improvement which finds majority support in Parliament.

Parliament, as a forum for debate, will be used by the Opposition to set out their views and policies so that the public, who will be asked to elect them at the next General Election, know what they are.

The Opposition also scrutinises the Executive and to enable it to do that effectively, it will appoint its own shadow cabinet of specialist spokesmen who will shadow the Ministers to whom they have been assigned. By these means, the shadow cabinet will build up experience and knowledge of some (but not all) of the important issues of Government. In this way they can be thought of as almost a 'Government in waiting', ready to take over at a moment's notice (that is all that they will have) if they are successful at the next General Election.

Parliamentary Standards

MPs, because of their representative rôle, come under a great deal of pressure. There are organisations whose sole purpose it is to lobby Ministers and MPs on behalf of their paying clients – to seek to influence Government and legislation in Parliament. Some MPs will be sponsored or may be retained as Parliamentary advisers by particular organisations – often involving payment to the MP.

There are obvious difficulties in this, because conflicts of interest can exist which are not readily apparent. So, over the last few years, Parliament has introduced a range of procedures aimed at preventing such conflicts of interest or at least bringing them out into the open.

The Commons maintains a public *Register of MPs' Interests* – financial, and some non-financial. An MP with a relevant interest must declare that interest when speaking in the House or committee, and must disclose it when giving notice of a question or motion. Similar disclosures must be made during any other proceedings in the House and in any dealings with Ministers, civil servants or other MPs.

Failure by particular MPs to do this was one of the features of the notorious *'cash for questions'* affair, in which allegations were made that certain MPs had received undisclosed cash and other benefits in return for asking specific questions in Parliament.

In November 1995, the Lords agreed to set up a similar *Register of Interests* for its members.

In 1995, the Commons went further and banned MPs from acting as advocates for any issue which was related to the source of any of their financial interests.

Also in 1995, the first *Parliamentary Commissioner for Standards,* Sir Gordon Downey, was appointed. This initiative followed the recommendations of the Committee on Standards in Public Life under Lord Nolan – known as the *Nolan Committee*. The Commissioner's rôle is to advise MPs on issues to do with standards and to undertake a preliminary investigation into complaints of alleged breaches of rules by MPs. His report on the outcome of his investigation is presented to the House of Commons Select Committee on Standards and Privileges.

His first big test was the *'cash for questions'* affair and although his report was complete, it remained unpublished because he could not present it to the Select Committee due to the dissolution of Parliament for the 1997 General Election, which some people suggested was unusually early. As a consequence, *'sleaze'* continued to be a General Election issue.

Abolition or Reform of the House of Lords

The issue of what to do about the House of Lords has been under discussion for many years. Indeed, the preamble to the Parliament Act 1911 envisaged an elected chamber – an objective which still has to be achieved.

Those who oppose the existence of the House of Lords and want to see its abolition, object to it for several reasons. Some feel that it is not representative – because many of its members are there by accident of birth rather than by democratic election and additionally they are drawn from an unrepresentative section of Society, likely to have an affinity with the Conservative Party. However, there are some who believe that more recent experience in the 1980s and 1990s suggests that the House of Lords was increasingly prepared to demonstrate its willingness to challenge Conservative Government legislation – explained as being due to the increasing number of life peers and a general change in attitude of its members, of whatever kind.

The composition of the House of Lords has been significantly altered over the years, by the inclusion of Life Peers appointed on merit – moving away from the principle of hereditary membership. The powers of the House of Lords to thwart the legislative will of the Commons has been severely curtailed. Both these points are discussed in more detail earlier in this chapter.

It is said that the limits now placed on the Lords are consistent with the belief that the legislative job of the non-elected House should be one of revision – complementing rather than rivalling the elected House. Certainly, the Lords has provided the Government with a useful second sounding board to correct and adjust Bills which might have been poorly drafted. Even the Lords' rejection of a Bill can provide a useful breathing space for further thought.

So, if a second legislative chamber is seen to have a useful function as a check on the work of the first chamber, then perhaps what is needed is reform rather than abolition. Reform could be as simple as removing the voting rights of the hereditary peers – or it could be as complex as reconstituting the Lords (with a change of name?) into a wholly or largely elected second chamber – or anything in between.

Many thought that the reform of the House of Lords would be high on the agenda of the New Labour Government following the 1997 General Election. But the first Queen's Speech of the new Parliament contained no reference to it as an issue requiring legislative attention in the first Session. Whether the issue gains more priority will emerge only in subsequent Queen's Speeches. One of the issues which will be addressed in the first Session is the control of handguns, in the wake of the Dunblane Massacre; it is said that the Bill to give effect to this will be fiercely opposed in the Lords. If that is the case and the Bill is delayed, then that might provide the catalyst which brings reform of the House of Lords to the top of the political agenda.

As it happens, the size of the Labour Party majority in the Commons after the 1997 General Election may well strengthen the arguments in favour of retaining a second chamber, however constituted. Some argue that a Government with a majority of 179 in the Commons could easily become an elected monarchy or oligarchy – rather strong words which probably underestimate the moderating influence of the Commons back bench MPs of all parties described earlier.

CHAPTER 3

The Government

The Prime Minister – the Cabinet – Ministers – Government Departments – the Civil Service

The Government

The Government is the Prime Minister and a group of Ministers who are collectively responsible for managing the national affairs of the UK in the name of the Sovereign.

The composition of the Government will vary from time to time, in terms of the number of Ministers and their titles. New Ministerial offices can come into existence and existing ones disappear; and functions can be shuffled around among Ministers by the Prime Minister.

Ministers may have responsibilities for a particular Government department or may hold one of the more formal non-departmental offices with little responsibilities, so that they can then concentrate on other specific areas of activity in support of the Government.

Ministers have been appointed from amongst the people sitting in Parliament for some time. It suited the Sovereign for his or her Ministers to be in Parliament so that they could exert influence for him or her over Parliament. The arrangement also suited Parliament because the Ministers could more easily be held to account for their actions if they were sitting in Parliament.

This practice has now become a convention and, furthermore, the convention has evolved so that it is generally the case that Ministers are drawn from the Commons. This makes the Commons more powerful in that it is the main route to Ministerial office. The fact that Ministers remain MPs means that they are readily accessible to and can be waylaid by the back bench MPs in the Commons, and they retain an affinity with back benchers since, even as Ministers, they still retain their constituency responsibilities.

The convention is also that Ministers will remain in post only if they remain in Parliament. If a Minister ceases to be an MP, they will usually lose office, unless special arrangements are made to preserve their position – either elevation to the House of Lords or arranging for the vacation of a safe seat to which they can be quickly elected.

Not more than 95 holders of Ministerial office are entitled to sit and vote in the Commons at any one time, presumably as a safeguard to preserve a sensible balance between the Executive and back bench MPs.

There will usually be several Ministers drawn from members of the Lords, even though its legislative powers have been reduced. The reason for this is that it suits the Government to have someone in that House able to muster support for it when it matters and to answer questions on its behalf there.

Some of the Ministers will be members of the Cabinet. However, it is sometimes the case that there is a small group of advisers around the Prime Minister who are not always members of the Cabinet and may not even be Ministers. Such a group can have a significant influence on the development of Government policy. These people are often referred to as the *'Kitchen Cabinet'* – a term first used in America during President Andrew Jackson's administration in 1830 to describe that kind of arrangement.

The Prime Minister

The Cabinet was originally chaired by the Sovereign. However, that changed when the Elector of Hanover came to Britain to become George I. He could speak little or no English and was not particularly interested in politics. So, the job of chairing the Cabinet was given to the *First Lord of the Treasury*, Sir Robert Walpole. Walpole took advantage of this to become the most important of the Sovereign's Ministers – the prime or first Minister – during the 1721-24 Government. The office of Prime Minister is generally regarded as starting at that period.

These days, the Sovereign appoints as Prime Minister the MP sitting in the Commons who leads the party with a majority of seats there. It is this political support in the Commons, together with the power to recommend the Sovereign to appoint and dismiss Ministers, which provides the basis of the Prime Minister's own authority.

The Prime Minister is, by tradition, *First Lord of the Treasury* and *Minister for the Civil Service*. The formal office of Prime Minister is unpaid; it is the other offices which produce the Prime Minister's salary.

The phrase *'Primus inter pares'* (First amongst Equals) is used in some textbooks to describe the nature of the Prime Minister's relationship with the other Ministers. In practice, that theoretical definition has to be considered in the light of the personal character and determination of the particular occupant of the office – which can result in various styles of leadership, ranging from a consensus style to one which is more directive or even Presidential.

The Prime Minister's Office is at 10 Downing Street which is also his or her official residence in London and the base for the Cabinet Office. There is a house in the country – Chequers – which is also available to the Prime Minister.

In addition to the Cabinet Office, the Prime Minister also has a Private Office in which is based the Prime Minister's Principal Private Secretary and a group of civil servants. Depending upon the character of the individual concerned, some members of the Private Office can become prominent in the public eye – Sir Bernard Ingham, Margaret Thatcher's Press Secretary is a recent example of this.

The rôle of the Prime Minister

The most important functions of the Prime Minister are to: chair meetings of the Cabinet; appoint and allocate work to Cabinet committees; oversee the work of the Government; and allocate functions to Ministers. He or she also keeps the Sovereign informed of Government business conducted in the Sovereign's name, during a weekly audience with the Sovereign. The Prime Minister is also Minister for the Civil Service.

There are other responsibilities of the Prime Minister in relation to appointments – including recommending whom the Sovereign should appoint as: Church of England Archbishops, bishops and deans; the Lord High Commissioner to the General Assembly of the Church of Scotland; Senior Judges, including the Lord Chief Justice; Privy Councillors; Lords-Lieutenant; and Poet Laureate and Constable of the Tower. There are also appointments to many public corporations (such as the BBC) which are made on the recommendation of the Prime Minister.

As explained in previous chapters, the Prime Minister also makes recommendations to the Sovereign for the conferment of most honours and peerages.

Constraints on the Prime Minister

The sources of the Prime Minister's authority mentioned above are also the sources of the constraints upon him or her. Even if the Prime Minister appears to be a strong personality, he or she is still not able to follow personal whim in a way which does not command support – or not for very long.

One of the bases of the Prime Minister's position is as the leader of the party which has a majority of members in the House of Commons – members who can be expected to vote for the Government's proposals. It follows that the individual can no longer continue as Prime Minister if the Parliamentary party decides that it would like a new leader or if the back bench members are not prepared to vote consistently in support of the Government in the Commons.

The Prime Minister needs to pay continual attention to maintaining a proper dialogue with the back benchers in order to be confident of their continued support – even if the Parliamentary majority is significant. It becomes even more crucial if that majority is slim. So, a sensible Prime Minister will take pains to keep the 1922 Committee or the Parliamentary Labour Party (as the case may be) fully informed and will be prepared to take into account their views. *Prime Minister's Question Time* is, perhaps, a more tangible example of a constraint upon the Prime Minister by back benchers in the Commons itself.

The other basis of the Prime Minister's authority is the ability to recommend the appointment and require the resignation of Ministers. The Government will work effectively only if the Ministers maintain their collective responsibility and pull in the same direction. The breadth of modern government is too great for the Prime Minister to do it all, so he or she has to rely upon the contributions from Ministers.

Any group of Ministers will contain a range of personalities, some strong, who will have their own responsibilities to protect and may have their own personal agendas. It makes sense for a Prime Minister to have a Cabinet which reflects the range of ideological ideas amongst the senior MPs. Apart from improving the quality of the decision-making at Cabinet level (and improving the chances of back bench support for Cabinet decisions), this also can have the advantage of stifling dissent (not always successfully) by fixing the people concerned with the convention of Collective Responsibility!

If the support of Ministers for the Prime Minister starts to weaken, then that will soon become evident (they may leak it themselves) and raise question marks about the future of the Prime Minister. In other words, there will come a point when the maxim *'Primus inter Pares'* really does count for something after all, regardless of the Prime Minister's own strength of character. Once uncertainties about continued support for the Prime Minister arise amongst the Ministers, those uncertainties will rapidly be brought to the notice of the back benchers and will tend to accelerate the momentum for change.

The fate of Margaret Thatcher is a case in point which illustrates both of these constraints in action. It became widely known that she had begun to ride roughshod over Cabinet decisions, making up her own policy as she went along, and this was not liked. This aspect of her leadership style came in for particular criticism from Sir Geoffrey Howe in his resignation speech to the Commons in November 1990 (see the later section on Collective Responsibility), which is generally regarded as dealing a fatal blow to Margaret Thatcher as Prime Minister.

In the subsequent fight for the leadership of the Conservative Party – which she lost – many of her Cabinet colleagues had told her privately that they thought that she would lose the second ballot – an indication of their loss of confidence in her. In addition, many in the Parliamentary party believed that they would lose the next General Election if she remained the party leader. She was forced to vacate 10 Downing Street, clearly bitterly disappointed, in favour of her successor John Major.

Secretaries and Ministers

There are various kinds of Minister in the Government. After the Prime Minister, the most senior are the *Secretaries of State* – or to give them their proper title, *Her Majesty's Principal Secretaries of State.* Constitutionally, Secretaries of State are regarded as the channel of communication between the Sovereign and the people and, by convention, the more important of them are appointed at a meeting of the Privy Council, where they signify their acceptance of office by kissing the Sovereign's hands.

Secretaries of State have responsibility for the major Government departments and are always members of the Cabinet. Secretaries of State are usually called *'Secretary of State'*, or *'Secretary'*, but some have special titles – *The Chancellor of the Exchequer or President of the Board of Trade,* for example.

The next most senior type of Minister is *Minister of State.* A Minister of State is a Minister who does not have responsibility for a Government department. However, such a Minister is often found in the larger departments, supporting the relevant Secretary of State and even taking responsibility for supervising a part of the department's work.

A Minister of State is not usually (but can be) a member of the Cabinet.

Again, some Ministers of State have special titles – *[Lord] President of the Council, the Chancellor of the Duchy of Lancaster, the Lord Privy Seal* and *the Paymaster General* are the usual examples. Occasionally, there will be a Minister of State called *Minister without Portfolio* – in other words, a Minister who, unlike the others, has been given no portfolio of responsibilities.

The purpose of those Ministers of State who are not based in a Government department is to undertake other work for the Government given to them by the Prime Minister. They can sometimes be much more influential than their title suggests. For example, Peter Mandelson (popularly referred to as the Labour Party's 'Spin Doctor') was appointed by Tony Blair as Minister without Portfolio *"to assist in the strategic implementation of government policies and their effective presentation to the public"*. Although he is not a member of the Cabinet, he will sit on all of its committees and be attached to the Cabinet Office and liaise with the Downing Street Policy Unit.

The lowest level of Minister is usually referred to as a *Junior Minister*, although they can still often have the title of 'Minister', with or without a further description in brackets to explain their responsibilities – all very confusing! Such Ministers are appointed to assist the more senior Ministers in their departmental work and are not members of the Cabinet. Their proper title depends upon the status of the departmental Minister whose work they support. If the senior Minister in the department is a Secretary of State, then the Junior Minister will be a *Parliamentary Under-Secretary of State*. If, however, the senior Minister they assist is not a Secretary of State, then the junior Minister is called *Parliamentary Secretary* and is likely to have a mix of Parliamentary and departmental duties.

To complete the picture, mention should be made here of *Parliamentary Private Secretaries* – even though they are not Secretaries or Ministers in any of the senses used so far in this section. These are MPs who are appointed, with no additional salary, to support the political work of a Minister in his or her Parliamentary liaison with other back bench MPs. Presumably the people concerned are prepared to take on these responsibilities as the first rung on the ladder to Ministerial office. They should not be confused with the Minister's *Private Secretary* who is a civil servant provided to support the work of the Minister as a Minister of the Crown.

Deputy Prime Minister

The title *First Secretary and Deputy Prime Minister* is a fairly recent one (created July 1995) and, in a way, is slightly at odds with the concept of 'Primus inter Pares'. What was novel was the *'First Secretary'* part of the title – there had been *'Deputy Prime Minister's* before – George Brown was one notable example. What was intended by having a *'First Secretary'* in relation to a Prime Minister was never clearly understood and the title was hardly ever referred to; it has not survived the 1997 General Election.

As far as a 'Deputy Prime Minister' is concerned, the relationship between that office and the other Ministers is also difficult to describe. Commentators often speculate upon the reason why the Prime Minister felt it necessary to concede that kind of power to the individual – consolation prize in a party leadership election, perhaps?

The Deputy Prime Minister is likely to have wide-ranging responsibilities simply because the job is ill-defined, but the precise rôle will probably depend upon the interests of the person concerned and their inclination to involve themselves in the work of the other Ministers.

The first, and only, occupant of the office of First Secretary and Deputy Prime Minister was Michael Heseltine and some commentators suggested that the creation of the post had a lot to do with the fight for the leadership of the Conservative Party and with the need to keep that party together thereafter. Apart from any general responsibilities (similar to those recently allocated by Tony Blair to Peter Mandelson, Minister without Portfolio), his interests lay in Trade and Industry – reflecting his former position as *President of the Board of Trade* – a title which he had revived for the office which had in recent years been called the *Secretary of State for Trade and Industry*.

The office of Deputy Prime Minister has survived the 1997 General Election, since it still exists and is now occupied by John Prescott. However, the rôle of the office seems to have changed, since it is combined with Environmental issues – John Prescott's formal title is *Deputy Prime Minister and Secretary of State for the Environment, Transport and the Regions*.

The 1997 New Labour Government

The composition of the New Labour Government which came into office following the 1997 General Election is set out in Appendix A, together with the salaries which can be claimed. Excluding the Whips' Office there is a total of 89 people in the Government.

The main new features are the elevation of the Overseas Development Administration to Department status (Secretary of State for International Development) and the creation of a Superministry under the Deputy Prime Minister (Secretary of State for the Environment, Transport and the regions)

The composition and rôle of the Cabinet

The Cabinet on average comprises about 20 Ministers selected by the Prime

Minister and occupies a central position in the political system. The size of peacetime Cabinets in the 20th century has ranged from 16 (Bonar Law 1922) to 24 (Wilson 1964). The Blair 1997 Cabinet consists of 22 people.

The rôle of the Cabinet is to:

- initiate and decide upon the Government's policy;

- control the Government; and

- co-ordinate the Government departments.

In other words, the Cabinet is the place where major decisions on policy are made or, more likely, proposals from its committees are ratified and where conflicts between Government departments are resolved.

The Cabinet meets on Thursday each week for about three hours while Parliament is in session and at other times if the Prime Minister so wishes.

The Cabinet Office consists of the Cabinet Secretariat and the Office of Public Service. The practice of keeping minutes of Cabinet decisions was introduced in 1916 by Lloyd George – and this led to the system which exists today – the Cabinet Secretariat. The Cabinet Secretary is also the Head of the Home Civil Service (reflecting one of the Prime Minister's paid offices: Minister for the Civil Service). The two rôles may, however, be split when the present incumbent, Sir Robin Butler, retires.

Votes are rarely taken in the Cabinet – to preserve the concept of Cabinet collective responsibility, the Prime Minister sums up his or her view of the conclusion of a discussion and this then becomes the decision of the Cabinet, recorded as such in the minutes. Just as the Cabinet meetings are secret, so are the minutes, although they may become eligible for later publication as public records under the 30 year rule. In spite of that, insights into the processes within the Cabinet, sometimes quite detailed, can often be gained from the published diaries of ex-Cabinet Ministers!

Cabinet government does have its critics: Ministers are often generalists, or are appointed to offices for which they have little previous experience (Jack Cunningham's appointment as Minister for Agriculture, Fisheries and Food by Tony Blair is a recent example).

Shuffling Ministers between jobs is also viewed as a mixed blessing. Some people believe that it can take a Minister about two years to understand their job fully; on the other hand, others argue that moving Ministers around stops them from 'going native'!

Finally, Ministers are often so overloaded with their departmental responsibilities that they cannot afford the time to consider, properly, any of the wider topics which come up from the Cabinet committees for Cabinet approval.

Cabinet committees

The complexity of modern government has led, inevitably, to overload on members of the Cabinet or to issues requiring more detailed consideration than can be accommodated at Cabinet meetings. So, a partial solution to the problem is the Cabinet committees, which are also bound by secrecy and are supported by the Cabinet Secretariat. There are three general types: standing, *ad hoc* or ministerial.

Standing committees are permanent and appointed for the duration of the Premiership; *ad hoc committees* exist to look at specific issues and are disbanded when their job is done; and *ministerial committees*, rather confusingly, consist only of civil servants.

Collective responsibility

Strictly speaking, the Cabinet in its executive rôle is deciding what advice to give the Sovereign in the government of the country. The convention is that the advice is *always unanimous* – in other words, every member of the Cabinet is expected to support a collective Cabinet decision even if he or she disagrees with it. Any differences of opinion are to be kept secret within the Cabinet itself. If the Minister refuses to accept or later opposes the Cabinet decision, he or she is expected to resign. In recent years the convention has been extended to all Junior Ministers, and even to the unpaid and unofficial Parliamentary Secretaries. That is the theoretical position on what is termed *Collective Responsibility*.

In reality, matters are different. There can be times when the convention of collective responsibility is formally relaxed by the Prime Minister – as Harold Wilson did in 1975 for the EEC referendum, where the Cabinet was split. In recent years, the convention has been unofficially breached on occasions, but without the corresponding resignation. Quite often the breach appears by a Minister leaking Cabinet discussions to highlight his or her disagreement with the Cabinet decision – as happened in 1986 when the Brittan/Heseltine disagreement over Westland Helicopters was widely reported in the media. There are other examples.

The practice has not been confined to Ministers – Margaret Thatcher herself had a tendency to depart from Cabinet decisions, especially on Europe, as explained by Sir Geoffrey Howe in his resignation speech:

"The task has become futile ... of trying to pretend there was a common policy when every step forward risked being subverted by some casual comment or impulsive answer [by Mrs Thatcher]".

Ministerial Responsibility

As already explained, Ministers can have departmental responsibilities. There is a convention, known as *Ministerial Responsibility*, which requires a Minister to accept responsibility to Parliament for his or her own personal conduct; the general conduct of the department for which he or she has responsibility; and the policy-related actions or omissions of his or her civil servants. The theory is that if a serious event of that kind occurs, then the expectation is that the Minister concerned will resign.

Again, in reality matters can be different. The best recent example of a Minister doing the 'decent thing' was Lord Carrington when he resigned (together with two other Ministers) as Foreign Secretary when Argentina invaded the Falklands – some might argue that the event was so serious that the Prime Minister herself should have resigned.

However, there have been other examples where a Minister has not resigned when most people considered that resignation was amply justified – instead, pragmatism has become the more important consideration. The best example of this was Norman Lamont who defended the UK's membership of the Exchange Rate Mechanism (ERM), only for the UK to be forced to withdraw in September 1992 after a disastrous run on the Pound, on 'Black Wednesday' which threatened a melt-down in the economy. By any objective standard Mr Lamont should have resigned immediately from the Treasury – but he didn't, presumably because this would have reflected badly on the quality of Cabinet government. He was, however, fired some time later and, like Sir Geoffery Howe, used his 'resignation' speech to criticise the style of the leadership of the Government.

The advent of the semi-independent (but still departmental) Agencies within Government departments has muddied the waters even more. Some cynics would say that the Agencies now provide a Minister with the ideal situation: the Minister can still play an influential part, unofficially, in the direction of the Agency and yet avoid responsibility when things go wrong, by claiming that the fault was an administrative or 'operational' one by the Agency, rather than a policy fault for which he or she should take responsibility.

Some would say that such a distinction is not envisaged by the convention; others would argue that it is now unrealistic to expect a Minister to take responsibility for literally everything which happens in the department or any of its executive agencies. An example of this is the catalogue of serious short-comings in the Prison Service which resulted in the eventual dismissal of Derek Lewis as the Director-General of the Prison Service (for which he won £220,000 damages for wrongful dismissal in the settlement of his High Court action against the Home Secretary). Many people felt at the time that Michael Howard should have resigned as Home Secretary under the convention of Ministerial Responsibility – but he didn't, arguing that he did not interfere in the running of the Prison Service and that the faults were 'operational' and not his responsibility.

Ann Widdicombe's May 1997 speech to the Commons about Michael Howard has already been mentioned *(see the section on back benchers in the previous chapter)*. Her comments included: *"We demean our high office if we mistreat our public servants. We demean ourselves if we come to this House and indulge in a play of words which ... may be unsustainable."*

Some commentators would now argue, with some justification, that resignation in accordance with the convention of Ministerial Responsibility has to all intents and purposes disappeared – or will only be honoured if the short-coming can be shown to have been the direct personal responsibility of the Minister concerned.

Government departments

The day-to-day work of government is done not by Ministers but by Government departments, staffed by civil servants, under Ministerial supervision. In other words, government is actually delivered by civil servants (as permanent managers of their departments) rather than by Ministers (temporary politicians in titular charge of a department). Government departments are accountable to Parliament through their supervising Secretary of State or Minister.

One of the most striking features of UK government is that although a complete change of government is more or less instantaneous after a General Election, the actual day-to-day work of government seems to go on without much interruption. This can be due to the shadow cabinet arrangement in which the members of the new Government are able to gain experience of the work of government and build up links with the senior staff of the Civil Service.

However, the ease with which the transition from one government to another takes place is largely due to the existence of the Civil Service, the staff of which are unaffected by a change in government in managing the delivery of government services. The similar transition of power in the USA is altogether more lengthy and traumatic. However, there may be straws in the wind suggesting a change in approach here *(see the later section 'Civil Servants – non-political?')*

'Whitehall' is the term usually applied to the government departments as a whole, but it is more properly applied to the central departments, the Great Offices of State: The Foreign and Commonwealth Office, the Home Office and Her Majesty's Treasury.

There are others which still retain the word *'Office'* in their title: the Northern Ireland, Scottish and Welsh Offices. Others still preserve the word *'Ministry'* in their titles; the Ministries of Defence and Agriculture, Fisheries and Food.

The remainder usually have the word *'Department'* in their title: Department of Health and the Department of the Environment, for example. Over time, the name of a Department can change as its functions change: for example the Department of Education and Science (DES) became the Department for Education (DfE) and is now the Department for Education and Employment (DfEE).

Some departments, like the Ministry of Defence, cover the whole of the UK. Others, such as the Department of Social Security, cover the UK with the exception of Northern Ireland. The Department of the Environment is primarily concerned with England.

Many departments have some sort of regional presence. The 10 Government Offices for the Regions look after the regional programmes of the Departments of the Environment, Trade and Industry, Education and Employment, Transport and of the Home Office.

Departments are usually headed by Ministers, but some can be headed by civil servants who are accountable to Parliament through a designated Minister – for example, the Ministers in the Treasury are responsible for the Inland Revenue, HM Customs and Excise and a number of other departments and agencies.

A list of current (1997) government departments and the more significant of their related agencies is set out in Appendix B.

The Civil Service

Civil servants are servants of the Crown – or, more realistically, the servants of the Government of the day. The Civil Service does not have, in constitutional terms, a separate existence from the Government.

The Civil Service is the ultimate responsibility of the Prime Minister in his or her capacity as Minister for the Civil Service and is the ultimate management responsibility of the Cabinet Secretary, as Head of the Home Civil Service.

The modern Civil Service has a long history and is still changing to reflect modern conditions. The principles underlying it have their origin in the Northcote-Trevelyan Report of 1854 which aimed to put the civil service on a more professional and neutral footing, after years of corruption and nepotism.

All appointments are made on merit by fair and open competition – one of the objectives of the Northcote-Trevelyan Report, which took some time to achieve after 1854. The independent Civil Service Commissioners are responsible for selecting people for the Senior Civil Service via the Civil Service Selection Board. The responsibility for recruiting all other staff rests with the department or agency itself – this can be done within the department/agency, by using private consultants or by using the Government's Recruitment and Assessment Services Agency. Since 1995, departments and agencies have been obliged to publish their recruitment arrangements.

The various grades of the Senior Civil Service and examples of the kind of work that they do are:

new	old	example of responsibility
1	Permanent Secretary	heads a major department
1A	Second Permanent Secretary	heads a smaller department/policy unit
2	Deputy Secretary	directs a large executive agency
3	Under Secretary	heads a functional division
4	[professional title]	holds a senior professional office
5	Assistant Secretary	heads a policy programme section
6	Senior Principal	heads a regional office
7	Principal	heads a local service office

Senior Civil Servants are encouraged to gain experience of industry and other areas of activity in order to broaden their personal skills. Similarly, exchanges of senior staff between central and local government also take place.

Civil Servants – non-political?

There can be interesting arguments surrounding the interaction between Ministers and their senior civil servants – about the extent to which each can be drawn into the other's theoretical area of responsibility.

The dividing line between policy (the Minister's preserve) and execution of that policy (the rôle of the civil servant) is not as clear-cut as some people like to think.

In recent years some Ministers have become much more active in the work of their departments – evidenced by Michael Heseltine's introduction in the early 1980s of MINIS (the Management Information System for Ministers) into the departments for which he was responsible. This can raise the suspicion that individual Ministers are more prepared to interfere in the management of the department, past the level required to discharge their accountability to Parliament.

In the other direction, there was uncertainty about the obligations owed by a civil servant to a Minister, which came to a head in the trial of Clive Ponting in 1985 for passing classified information to an unauthorised person under the Official Secrets Act. Although Ponting was acquitted, this led to Sir Robert Armstrong (the Cabinet Secretary and Head of the Civil Service at the time) issuing a 'Note' emphasising that:

> *"The determination of policy is the responsibility of the Minister ... When, having been given all the relevant information and advice, the Minister has taken the decision, it is the duty of civil servants loyally to carry out that decision ... Civil servants are under an obligation to keep the confidences to which they become privy in the course of their official duties."*

That was in 1985. Since then, 'whistle-blowing' has become a more acceptable occupation if the circumstances demand that exposure of malpractice is in the public interest.

A White Paper, *The Civil Service: Continuity and Change*, was published in 1994 and discussed the rôle and future of the Civil Service. This led to the publication of a new Civil Service Code which came into force in January 1996. The Code provides a statement of the constitutional framework within which all civil servants work and the values which they are expected to uphold. The Code also includes an independent line of appeal to the Civil Service Commissioners on alleged breaches of the Code.

As explained in the last section, appointments are to be made by fair and open competition. However, over the last few years, the number of 'political advisers' in Whitehall, paid for out of public funds, has increased – to 38 towards the end of the Major government. The Blair Government has now increased this number to 53, with 18 in the Prime Minister's Office. Opinions differ about this – modern political reality (how can 450,000 civil servants be politicised by so few?); or the thin end of the wedge (towards the USA model without proper debate by Parliament?).

Political activities of civil servants

Civil servants are expected to implement the decisions of the Government of the day, regardless of their own privately-held political beliefs and convictions – this is said to be a matter of public confidence in the political impartiality of the Civil Service. This does not mean, however, that civil servants are denied altogether the freedom to take part in the democratic political process which is enjoyed by others.

So, there is a set of internal rules which divides the Civil Service into three groups to determine the extent to which an individual civil servant can engage in political activity on a personal basis.

At one end is the 'politically free' group (mostly industrial or the non-office grades) who are free to engage in political activity, including standing as an MP or MEP. At the other end there is a 'politically restricted' group, consisting of staff in Grades 7 and above, Administration Trainees and Higher Executive Officers (D) who are banned from taking part in national political activities but who can apply for permission to engage in politics at a local level. In between is the 'intermediate' group (everyone else) who can apply for permission to engage in political activity at national and local level, but who cannot stand as MPs or MEPs.

Departmental Management

The Civil Service has undergone a marked change in the last 20 years as a result of a series of management reforms aimed at providing the *'three Es'* – economy, efficiency and effectiveness.

There were two main milestones on this journey to more effective management. The *Efficiency Strategy* published in 1979 by Sir Derek (later Lord) Rayner, who was the Prime Minister's adviser on efficiency, started the process. In 1982 this impetus for change was reinforced by the *Financial Management Initiative* which sought to provide departmental managers with *"a clear view of objectives and performance"*.

More recent developments took the process one stage further, by transferring as much as possible of the executive work of Government departments to separate executive units or agencies under the *Next Steps Programme* initiated in 1988.

This programme was mainly driven by the view that the volume of Government services and the size of departments had become so large that management and supervision of them as single entities was no longer sensible. There was also the view that middle-ranking managers would be better able to develop the services which they managed, if they had more flexibility by being freed from hierarchical control by the centre of their department. It was also intended as the possible route to privatisation – and some of the next steps agencies have taken that step.

Executive Agencies

Agencies created under the Next Steps Programme are still part of the Civil Service, but enjoy greater delegated freedom on finance and pay under their framework documents. Each agency is headed by a chief executive (the actual job title may be different and the post-holder will probably not be a career civil servant) who is responsible for the day-to-day operations of the agency but is accountable to the supervising Minister.

The Next Steps Programme envisages that an agency will not be created until some 'prior options' – abolition, privatisation or contracting-out – have been considered and rejected. These 'prior options' are also reviewed every five years once an executive agency has been established.

By the end of 1995, 366,000 civil servants (67% of the total) worked in executive agencies created under the Next Steps Programme.

Market testing

The process did not stop at the Next Steps Programme – it went further. The Conservative Government saw great value in the concept of the 'market place' and introduced a process for 'market testing', which can be viewed as an extension of the process of the privatisation of Government services.

The original idea was to improve efficiency and customer responsiveness by comparing the in-house provision (often in a monopoly position and remote from commercial pressures) with competitive bids from the private sector. The process of comparison would force the in-house provider to find the true cost of what they did and shake itself up, in order to keep the right to continue providing the service.

This concept had first appeared in the form of Compulsory Competitive Tendering (CCT) for certain blue-collar local government services in 1980. Its extension to the more significant parts of central government services was heralded in the Government's White Paper, *Competing for Quality*, published in 1991, promising that before the next election, 25% of certain kinds of departmental work would have been exposed to competition, affecting over 130,000 civil servants overall.

In principle, the process looks to be a sensible one, but other views can be made. The most important one is whether the service is to be awarded to the people who put in the lowest cash bid, regardless of the quality of the service they are likely to be able to deliver.

Supporters forget to take into account the costs of the necessary subsequent arms' length monitoring of the contractor's performance, when deciding whether the exercise has produced any worthwhile gain to the public purse. Another important point is the diversion of in-house resources and staff time (which is never truly costed) away from service delivery in order to compete in the market-testing process.

Finally there will sometimes be distrust or even hostility about the process, leading inevitably to an adverse effect on staff morale.

The Citizen's Charter

The changes described in the last few sections may have had other objectives, including improving the standard of services to the public, as well as controlling their cost and improving the way that they were managed. The 'customer focus' of public services (in their wider sense), however they were delivered, was made more explicit in John Major's *Citizen's Charter* announced in 1991.

The purpose of this initiative was to produce "a revolution in public services" by raising and emphasising the quality of service delivery. It covered all Government departments and agencies, the National Health Service, nationalised industries (since largely disappeared), privatised utilities, local government and the universities.

A set of public service principles was set out in the Citizen's Charter – under headings such as: standards, information and openness, choice and consultation, courtesy and helpfulness, putting things right, and value for money.

The programme is the responsibility of the Chancellor of the Duchy of Lancaster. The Chancellor is supported by the Citizen's Charter Unit within the

Office of Public Service in the Cabinet Office. There is also assistance from the Prime Minister's Citizen's Charter Advisory Panel which also judges the winners, whose achievement is rewarded by the Charter Mark of Excellence.

Quangos

Although by definition not part of government, this chapter would not be complete without a comment upon the growth of the Quango – *Quasi-autonomous Non-governmental Organisation*. Many people do not realise how many quangos there are and how much public expenditure they control – all with no direct democratic control.

The massive growth in the number of quangos was a feature of the last Conservative government. The more cynical would say that they were the means by which criticism of government policies would diminish if those responsible for overseeing the delivery of services were appointees of the government, rather than local democratically elected representatives.

Examples of quangos at local level are Training and Enterprise Councils, housing associations and grant-maintained school governing bodies. At national level, the chance is that any body with the word 'Authority' in its name is probably a quango.

The scale of quangodom is difficult to gauge (different commentators will give different values) but the following figures from a *Democratic Audit* report published in July 1996 give some idea:

- there are between 66,000 and 73,500 people running quangos;

- there are about 26,500 local councillors running local authorities;

- there are 6,224 executive and advisory quangos;

- quangos spent £60.4 billion in 1994/95, against a government estimate of £20.8 billion; and

- local authorities spent £73 billion in the same period.

The major point is the lack of accountability of quangos for what they do. The National Audit Office produced a report in June 1996 in response to a government consultation paper on the spending of public money published in the previous March. The NAO emphasised the need for proper audit and accountability of quangos for the public money they spent.

The NAO comment was consistent with the report published in May 1996 by the Nolan Committee on Standards in Public Life which included the following comments on quangos at local level:

> *"More needs to be done to ensure that they all achieve the best standards on appointments procedures, openness, codes of conduct, training, whistle-blowing and local accountability."*

Lord Nolan's letter to the Prime Minister which accompanied the report stressed:

> *"nothing ... points to any fundamental malaise in the sectors we have examined. But there is ... a tension between the management-driven and output-related approach which is central to many recent changes, and the need for organisations providing public services to involve, respond to, and reflect the communities which they serve."*

Will the New Labour Government increase accountability in line with the NAO and Nolan Committee comments?

CHAPTER 4

The Political Process

Pressure Groups – Political Parties

As explained in Chapter 1, the UK is a democracy. The political process within a democratic society is more than just participation in elections. Democracy is enhanced if individuals can express their views freely for a variety of causes – with the aim of influencing the views of other members of society and of those in government.

Pressure groups

Pressure groups are the means by which individuals seek to influence others. There are two main types of pressure group – a sectional or interest group, and a cause group.

Sectional or *interest groups* exist for the purpose of promoting and protecting the economic and other interests of their members. *Cause groups* exist to promote a much broader idea or issue which is not directly linked to the interests of their members.

Both types of pressure groups exist in the UK. Examples of sectional or interest groups are the various trade unions and professional societies and organisations representing the various sections of industry. Examples of cause groups are Greenpeace and CND.

Pressure groups vary enormously in their size and in the formality of their internal structure and organisation. At one end of the scale, there can be a fairly informal grouping of individuals with similar views on a single issue. At the other end, there can be large formalised organisations employing a significant number of people and with very substantial spending power (such as the CBI).

The more successful pressure groups will be those who follow the guidelines suggested by Des Wilson in 1986 during the Tyne Tees TV programme *Is Democracy working?*:

> *Identify your objectives; learn how the decision-making process works; formulate a strategy and campaign plan; undertake thorough and detailed research and preparation; mobilise as much widespread support as possible; understand how the mass media work and use them effectively; be professional; be confident about asserting your democratic rights; and be resilient and prepared for a long and difficult campaign.*

Pressure groups of whatever kind will seek to influence the legislative, government and political processes in much the same way.

Influencing others

Government will, more often than not, regard the influence of pressure groups in a positive, rather than negative, light. White and Green Papers are the more formal means by which views of pressure groups are sought in the legislative process. Although a pressure group's objectives may not match those of the legislature, nonetheless the knowledge and experience within the pressure group can be a valuable aid to the legislature. The end result is that the legislation, when passed, will work more correctly and efficiently to tackle the problem at which it is aimed.

The process of influencing government itself can be more subtle. The Executive has a wide discretion in the way it exercises its powers and pressure groups will seek to persuade those in government to use those powers in a way which is consistent with the group's aims and objectives. Ministers and civil servants are the more obvious targets, since they are part of the Executive. However, individual MPs, although properly speaking separate from the Executive, are also targeted because of the influence they can exert in monitoring the work of the Executive *(see Chapter 2 – section on backbenchers)*.

As a generalisation, the two aspects – legislative and governmental – come together in the political process itself. Many MPs will have some sort of connection with pressure groups. For example, many Labour MPs will be sponsored by a trade union. Many MPs (of any party) will be retained as paid or unpaid Parliamentary 'advisers' for pressure groups – providing those pressure groups with direct access to the legislative and governmental processes.

Influencing the political process raises at least two interesting issues: Firstly, the extent to which the connection between a pressure group and an MP is disclosed by the MP when he or she deals with or raises an issue. Secondly, the recent rapid growth in the number of lobbying organisations whose sole purpose is to influence the political process (through hospitality at which introductions and meetings are arranged) often for quite lucrative fees.

Political parties

The essential difference between a pressure group and a political party is simple to state: pressure groups exist to influence others, including those in government; political parties exist to take a direct part in the process of government itself.

Political parties will also differ from pressure groups in that their objectives will be bound up with a much broader set of ideas to do with Society generally. One practical result of this will be that the party membership will consist of a range of interests – a range which may be reflected in the internal organisation of the party itself, on a geographical or other basis.

In the UK there is a number of parties – three relatively large; the remainder relatively small. One must appreciate that sometimes a small party can exert much more influence on government policy than its size might suggest – especially if the government of the day needs the votes from that smaller party to survive in Parliament.

As far as Wales, Scotland and Northern Ireland are concerned, there are other much smaller parties in those countries with aims connected with ideas of national identity or religion. Those parties are often sufficiently successful, in electoral success, to defeat one or more of the larger parties. *(See Chapter 2, the House of Commons section, for the reflection of this in the 1997 General Election results).*

This kind of electoral success is, however, diluted in the wider UK Parliament. If Scotland gains its own Parliament and Wales its own Assembly, this might, in some ways, change, although how real that change would actually be will depend upon the extent of devolution.

Each of the three larger parties will now be described in terms of its development and internal organisation. In all three cases, the party's history has had a formative influence on the way it is organised.

The Conservative Party – development

The modern Conservative Party can be said to have its origins in Parliament itself – growing out of the old Tory Party during the middle of the last century. Indeed, people who are members of the Conservative Party still refer to themselves as being a 'Tory'. The initial preoccupation of the Tory Party was with supporting the established religious and political order, which also coincided with the interests of the landed classes. At that time, the landed classes were in a position to control a large number of MPs through the rotten borough system – but this was brought to an end by the Reform Act 1832.

As subsequent electoral reforms extended the franchise beyond the initial 5% of the population, so the Tory Party had to broaden its appeal downwards into the general population, if it was to retain its political position. In that sense, the development of the modern Conservative Party from the old Tory Party has been described as 'top-down'.

The Conservative Party – style of government

The modern Conservative Party has been in government for two-thirds of the time since 1918 and during that time has approached the business of government in different ways.

There have, in recent years, been tensions within the party. For many years during the 1960s and 1970s the Conservative leaders took care to position the party in the centre of the political spectrum – sometimes referred to as 'One-nation Conservatism'. They believed that there was a positive rôle for the State in providing welfare, full employment and taking care of the poorer and more vulnerable members of society.

However, the arrival of Mrs Thatcher as leader saw a significant shift to the right, towards a more 'radical reforming' or 'neo-liberal' type of Conservatism – 'Thatcherism'. This gave prominence to the concept of the free market, regarding the rôle of government as often unnecessary or obstructive for the health of the economy and, therefore, society.

Such Conservatism was prepared to accept a significant amount of unemployment and a reduction in public expenditure to a minimum, if that brought economic stability. The view was that people should themselves make provision to see them through adversity. One of the consequences of this type of Conservatism was the increasing polarisation of UK society into 'two nations' – the 'Haves' and the 'Have-nots'.

Loyalty to the leader is one of the features of the Conservative Party. However, that loyalty is not unquestioning. Even Mrs Thatcher was obliged to include in her Cabinet some people who were more inclined to support the greater public expenditure implications of the 'One-nation' approach – the so-called 'wets'.

Most political parties, if they are realistic, will reposition themselves in the political spectrum if they see this as the best way of making themselves more attractive to the voters – especially after a bad election result. The Labour Party did this after their defeat in the 1992 General Election (becoming 'New Labour' in the process), and the Conservative Party may attempt a similar process after their even worse defeat in 1997, once they have sorted out their leadership problems.

The Conservative Party – choosing the leader

Before 1965 there were no formal selection procedures for leader of the Conservative Party – the leader just 'emerged' when a Conservative government needed to be formed.

In 1965, the party adopted an approach in which Conservative MPs elect the leader from amongst their number following a secret ballot. In 1975, the process was modified so that the leader had to seek re-election annually – making it easier to dispose of a leader whose sell-by date had expired!

At present, the process is organised by the 1922 Committee. When there is a vacancy in the leadership, candidates must be nominated by two MPs. When there is no vacancy (a challenge to the existing leader), a candidate's nomination papers must be signed by at least 10% of the Parliamentary party. Balloting takes place five days after the close of nominations. During that five-day period, the views of Conservative constituency associations, MEPs and peers are collected by the 1922 Committee, although the result is still in the hands of the MPs themselves.

To win at the first ballot, a candidate needs to gain at least 50% of the votes and 15% more than any other candidate. If a winner is not produced the first time, a second ballot is run, but with the winner only needing at least 50% of the votes; at this stage, some of the less favoured candidates may withdraw and new candidates can enter the fray. If the second ballot does not produce a result, then a third ballot is run, involving only the top two candidates from the second ballot. If the third ballot produces a tie, then a fourth ballot is run, unless the two candidates concerned decide between themselves which of them will be the new leader.

This process may well change. The 1997 General Election debâcle produced several results – the resignation of John Major as leader; a delay in running the required leadership contest because most of the 1922 Committee (including its chairman) had lost their seats; and a call for the rules to be changed so that constituency representatives, MEPs and peers could take a more active part in voting for the choice of party leader.

The Conservative Party – organisation

Because of how the Conservative Party developed, the 1922 Committee is very influential. The Committee gets its name from a meeting in the Carlton Club in 1922 at which Conservative MPs persuaded Austin Chamberlain to pull out of a coalition with the Liberals.

The 1922 Committee represents Conservative backbench power in Parliament and any party leader who disregards it will usually regret doing so later.

Outside Parliament, the National Union of Conservative Associations ('National Union') was established in 1867 to co-ordinate the work of the local constituency associations. It has a Central Council, consisting of Conservative peers, MEPs, prospective MPs and regional representatives. The Central Council meets annually and its main job is to organise the party conferences.

The purpose of the Annual Conference of delegates from constituency associations is to inspire the party faithful, enable budding MPs to make their mark and provide advice to the party leadership from the grass-roots. The event is carefully orchestrated and provides a fairly anodyne public relations platform for the party leadership – especially the leader, who always receives a 10-minute standing ovation! In real terms, the Annual Conference has no rôle in policy formulation and it is difficult to guess how much notice the party leadership actually takes of what is said at the conference.

Central Office is the organisational core of the party. It is controlled by the party leader who appoints the Party Chairman and the several Vice-Chairmen who effectively run Central Office. Central Office co-ordinates the General Election campaign at national level and at other times provides policy advice and secretarial support to the leadership, through its Research Department, which was established in 1925. The work of the Research Department is now supplemented by the Advisory Committee on Policy, an influential body consisting of party representatives in Parliament and elsewhere.

A diagram showing the organisation of the Conservative Party appears at the end of this chapter.

The Conservative Party – choosing the Parliamentary candidates

The constituency associations operate at constituency level with the aim of winning or retaining the seat. The process which finishes with the selection of a person to be the Conservative Party candidate for the constituency operates at national and then local level.

At national level, there is a screening process through which hopefuls have to pass. This involves the National Union's Standing Advisory Committee and Parliamentary Selection Board vetting people for inclusion in the Approved List of Candidates. The process is run by Central Office and managed by one of the party's Vice Chairmen. The candidates have to survive a 'candidates weekend' at which they have to demonstrate the appropriateness of their personality and their political and other skills.

At local level, the process starts with a vacancy being notified to Central Office, which in turn tells people on the Approved List. Anyone from the Approved List who then applies may be short-listed (about 20 applicants) and vetted by the constituency association's Executive Sub-committee (about 20 constituency association officers). People who are not named on the Approved List can still be considered, but specific clearance by the Standing Advisory Committee is needed.

The Executive Sub-committee will usually reduce, through a process of interviews, the short-list to not less than three candidates. At this stage, the constituency association's Executive Council (about 60 constituency association officers) takes over and interviews the survivors, with the aim of offering at least two of them a final interview before the constituency association's General Meeting (all members of at least six months' standing).

Predictably, in safe seats the number of applications is usually high. As far as male candidates are concerned, the qualities of the candidate's partner appear to be equally important and they can sometimes tip the balance! Although loyalty to the sitting MP appears to be one of the tenets of the Conservative Party – at least in former times – in recent years constituency associations have shown themselves to be increasingly prepared to deselect a sitting MP if he or she has become an electoral liability.

Although the impression might be given that selection is a matter for the constituency association, occasionally the influence of Central Office can be seen in the final choice. Since 1948, the practice has stopped of according preference to those people willing to donate large sums of money to party funds.

Oddly enough, it is not necessary for a Conservative MP to be a member of the Conservative Party – as the party leadership discovered when they tried to expel Neil Hamilton after the damning report from the Parliamentary Commissioner, Sir Gordon Downey, into the 'cash for questions' affair – Hamilton was not a member and could not be expelled! That is likely to change and there is also a proposal for the keeping of a national list of disapproved (as well as approved) people.

The Conservative Party – finance

Individual constituency associations raise funds for their own activities and to meet a quota from Central Office for national funds. About 10% of national funds is raised in this way.

Traditionally, the larger companies made donations to the Conservative Party (which had to be listed in their annual accounts if they exceeded £200) but this source has diminished over the years. Money also flows into the party's coffers through a variety of sources, some of which are 'front' organisations set up for that purpose – such as Aims for Industry and British United Industrialists.

The source of the remainder is unclear. The party has steadfastly refused to disclose the sources of the largest part of its income – even when rumours have persisted of large cash donations from foreign businessmen (with the implication that secret influence was being sought). This may well change, because the New Labour Government has made one of its priorities the introduction of legislation requiring political parties themselves to publish the sources of their income.

The Labour Party – development

If the development of the modern Conservative Party can be described as 'top-down', the development of the Labour Party can be described as 'bottom-up'. The origins of the Labour Party are entirely different, evolving from a grass-roots movement outside Parliament.

In 1900 the trade unions, co-operative societies and socialist societies established the Labour Representation Committee to promote the entry of the working-class man into Parliament. The Committee changed its name to the Labour Party in 1906.

A written constitution was adopted in 1918. This constitution set out the party's objectives and the procedures for elections, appointments and decision-making within the party. The federal origins of the Labour Party are still evident in its modern structure – with its emphasis on the National Executive Committee and the Party Conference as the mechanisms by which party policy is developed. The pre-eminence of the Conservatives' 1922 Committee is not replicated in the Parliamentary Labour Party's position in the Labour scheme of things.

The Labour Party – approach to policy formulation

If the Conservative Party is traditionally regarded as the party of the *status quo*, the Labour Party is the party of change – either gradual or root-and-branch.

The Labour Party has formed the government for less than one-third of the time since 1918. This period in opposition has enabled the various interests within the party to assert themselves, with shifts towards the left and, more lately, towards the centre being made. Given the history of the party, and the breadth and ideological differences of its membership, it is hardly surprising that the party was much more prone to internal factions and divisions than the Conservatives – although in recent years the Conservative Party has itself been increasingly driven by internal divisions. Being leader of the Labour Party in opposition was probably one of the toughest jobs in UK politics!

The 1918 Constitution also set out the Labour Party's ideology and this tended to limit the ability of the Labour Party, in and out of government, to modify its aims and policies to meet the prevailing conditions of the day – until recently. The public ownership of the major utilities – including the steel and coal industries – was for many years a major feature of Labour policies – the 'clause four' issue.

The relative importance of the trade unions within the Labour Party became more evident during the so-called 'winter of discontent' in 1979 when the industrial action taken by the trade unions on the collapse of Labour's incomes policy resulted in the paralysis of most of the UK's industry.

There has always been a tension between the leadership and the National Executive Committee. The Labour Party rules provided for the NEC to control the formulation of future party policy; and they also provided for a resolution passed by a two-thirds majority at Annual Conference to become part of the election programme, but not part of the manifesto.

During the Wilson and Callaghan governments (1974-79) the respective Prime Ministers did not follow the path laid down by the NEC and the Annual Conference, with the result that they were dubbed 'revisionist' by some people in the party.

James Callaghan's style of government and his defeat at the 1979 General Election gave rise to disillusion and a split in the party. This enabled the hard left to gain significant influence within the NEC and at local level – at least for a time.

Neil Kinnock is generally credited with reversing the trend towards the left. By the mid 1980s he had secured the expulsion from the party of the supporters of *Militant Tendency*. He also restored the influence of the leader on the party machine and particularly on the NEC. By the time he took office as party leader, John Smith inherited a more centrally controlled party – the leadership was able to determine the party manifesto and election campaign.

The success of the Conservative Party in retaining the right to govern following their victory in the 1992 General Election caused the Labour Party to review the way in which it formulated policy. There is now a National Policy Forum (of about 150 to 200 members elected biannually at the Conference) which, through its seven standing commissions, has the job of producing policy proposals for Conference consideration. All aspects of party policy (including suggestions from constituency parties) are examined on a two-year rolling programme basis.

The success of the National Policy Forum approach to policy formulation can be seen in the repositioning of the Labour Party to become New Labour. The ideological differences between Marxists and liberal socialists appear to have largely disappeared – an apparently united party with a sure sense of direction has now evolved, more attractive to the voters. The state ownership of the means of production and socialism are no longer serious issues; nor is increasing taxation to increase public expenditure to generate jobs. The political complexion of the NEC has shifted back towards the centre of the spectrum – indeed, some would say even to the centre ground abandoned by the Conservatives when they adopted 'Thatcherism'.

Trade union leaders have seen their ability to influence the work of government through industrial action progressively diminish through a combination of rising unemployment and Conservative employment legislation. The voting power of the trade union leaders at the Annual Conference has also steadily been eroded (see later). In the past, trade unions have been portrayed as a having a close (some would say too close) relationship with a Labour government of the time. To counter this impression, in the run-up to the 1997 General Election Tony Blair made it clear that trade unions would not receive any special treatment from a New Labour government.

Perhaps there really is a new climate of political realism, but it remains to be seen whether Tony Blair will be more adept than his predecessors in managing his relationship with the NEC, the Annual Conference and the trade unions, when in government.

The Labour Party – choosing the leader

After the fall of the Callaghan government in 1979, the left wing increased its influence within the party with the aim of making it even more 'democratic' – in other words, moving control away from the leadership and the Parliamentary Labour Party and putting it firmly outside Parliament in the hands of the NEC.

This resulted in the 1981 Annual Conference changing the rules so that the leader of the party would be chosen in future not by MPs but by an electoral college. The electoral college now consists of three groups: the trade unions; the individual membership of the Labour Party; and Parliamentary Labour Party/European Parliamentary Labour Party – each college accounting for one-third of the votes.

Individual nominations still need a significant level of support from the Parliamentary Labour Party – 12.5% if there is a vacancy; 20% if there is no vacancy. Because of the electoral college system, voting is by means of postal ballot. The successful candidate needs at least 50% of the votes in each college. If no candidate has 50% at the first count, the lowest candidate is eliminated from the contest and the votes redistributed until a winner is identified.

The Labour Party – the NEC and the Annual Conference

The National Executive Committee is elected by the Annual Conference and runs the party's organisation. Its composition is:

12	elected by trade unions only
7	elected by OMOV postal ballot of all Labour Party members
5	women elected by the entire conference
1	Party Treasurer elected by the entire conference
1	elected by the socialist associations
1	leader of the Young Socialists ex-officio
1	leader of the Labour Party ex-officio
1	deputy leader of the Labour Party ex-officio

OMOV is the acronym for 'one member, one vote' – a concept which (as will be seen) is gaining increasing ground over the trade union 'block vote' within the decision-making processes of the Labour Party. The trade union block vote is wielded by trade union leaders on behalf of those members of their trade union who, as well as their union subscriptions, also pay the political levy to the Labour Party. These block votes collectively outweigh the votes of the smaller socialist societies and individual constituency members. In practice, the individual leaders of five of the largest unions – TGWU, AUEW, GMBATU, UNISON and USDAW – control a significant proportion of the votes.

The Annual Conference is altogether more lively than the Conservatives' equivalent and has a much more significant rôle in formulating party policy.

Issues will be debated, often with passion, and with the original proposal being substantially amended before the final vote. The leader of the party, unlike his or her Conservative opposite number, cannot usually expect an easy ride at the Annual Conference. However, there are signs that the New Labour leadership are looking at ways of reducing the emergence of internal party differences at the Annual Conference.

In an attempt to modernise the Labour Party, the NEC agreed in 1991 to reduce the unions' total voting strength from 90% to 70% of the total, after 1993 and to 40% over the long term, linked to a commensurate rise in party membership. A long-term aim of John Smith, before he died, was to see the end of the union block vote altogether and its replacement by OMOV at the Annual Conference. His aim is well on the way to being achieved:

	unions	constituencies
1994	90%	10%
1995	70%	30%
1996	50%	50%

but there is still some way to go.

The Labour Party – choosing the Parliamentary candidates

The left succeeded at the 1980 Annual Conference in securing the mandatory reselection of MPs during the lifetime of a Parliament. Some commentators argue that this made some moderate Labour MPs jump ship to the SDP when they realised that their position as sitting MP was under threat from the left at constituency level.

At constituency level, the trade unions had the power of a block vote at General Management Committee meetings in the selection of MPs and this tended to reinforce the view that the trade unions effectively controlled the party (through this and their block votes at the Annual Conference).

Neil Kinnock had tried, unsuccessfully, at the 1984 and 1987 Annual Conferences to introduce OMOV as the sole means of candidate selection. The 1987 Conference introduced a compromise involving shifting selection from the constituency General Management Committee to a local electoral college – individual members accounting for at least 60% of the votes, with the trade unions having the remainder. This compromise turned out to be very difficult and confusing to operate in practice and was not popular.

At the Annual Conference in 1993, John Smith tried again by proposing that trade union block voting in the selection of MPs should go completely. The new method would be OMOV, with a 'levy plus' system, under which trade union members paying the party levy could become full members of the Labour Party (and able to vote for themselves) by paying an extra £3.

Some trade union leaders regarded this as a threat to their influential position and were determined to stop it – with a good chance of success due to their block vote at the Annual Conference itself. The vote appeared to be finely balanced, with the unions more or less evenly divided on the issue, and the outcome was uncertain.

John Smith had put his reputation as leader on the line in trying to push this issue through – *"As the party of change we must surely be able to change ourselves"*. John Prescott is generally credited with just tipping the balance with a last-minute off-the-cuff speech – *"This man, our leader, put his head on the block by saying 'I fervently believe in a relationship and a strong one between the trades unions and the Labour Party'. He has put his head there; now it is time to vote. Give us a little trust."* This appeal won the day – but only just (47.5% for; 44.4% against).

The OMOV selection process, although more democratic than the system it replaced, has turned out to be somewhat more bureaucratic. The Labour Party maintains, like the Conservatives, a national list of approved candidates; the difference is that local constituency parties are not obliged to choose a candidate only from that source – although the person who emerges at the end of the selection process will still need NEC endorsement.

Prospective candidates have to have been members of the Labour Party for at least two years. They must be nominated by a 'nominating body' – ward and branch parties, affiliated trade unions and socialist societies, women's sections, Young Labour and the Executive of the Constituency Labour Party.

The General Management Committee of the Constituency Labour Party short-lists and then vets the hopefuls, who are required to write an election address of not more than 500 words.

If the constituency is already represented by a Labour MP, that person must be short-listed; and if that person is nominated by two-thirds of the nominating bodies, he or she is automatically re-selected and the process goes no further.

Any candidate receiving 25% of the nominations (must include one from a ward or branch party) is automatically short-listed. Guaranteed short-listing is also enjoyed by anyone receiving 50% of the nominations from affiliated organisations. The short-list should contain at least one woman.

The survivors of the General Management Committee stage move on to a

Selection Meeting of the whole Constituency Party at which there is an NEC observer and an OMOV ballot. The process is completed when the NEC endorses the preferred candidate. The NEC has greater influence at selection for a by-election, intervening at an earlier stage by approving the short-list.

The rôle of the NEC in candidate selection is important and can lead to disagreements with constituency parties which are intent on choosing someone who is regarded as unsuitable by the NEC – in the end, the NEC wins. In some instances, the NEC has even imposed its own candidate upon the local party.

In an earlier chapter reference was made to the results of the 1997 General Election and in particular to the increased number of women MPs, especially on the Labour benches. This was no accident. For a time, 1993 to 1996, the Labour Party practised positive discrimination in favour of women through the use of women-only (or 'closed') short-lists.

Initially the hope was that sufficient women-only short-lists would emerge through local consensus. In the event, progress was disappointing, so the NEC intervened by requiring specific constituency parties to adopt women-only short lists. This element of compulsion led to increasing disagreement and the practice was under review for termination after the next General Election. It had to stop in January 1996, anyway, when an Industrial Tribunal in Leeds declared the practice to be unlawful under the Sex Discrimination Act 1975.

The Labour Party – structure

The internal organisation of the Labour Party and the interrelationship of its various elements are complex and are best shown by means of the diagram which appears at the end of this chapter.

The Labour Party – finance

About half of the membership of the UK's trade unions pay a political levy as part of their union membership subscription. This is passed on to the Labour Party nationally and makes up about 80% of its finance. This explains, to some extent, the voting power of the trade unions.

The remainder of the party's finance is made up of membership subscriptions from individual members and from cash donations from companies and individuals.

The Liberal Democrats – development and policy

The Liberal Democrat Party as such is relatively recent, although the Liberal part goes back as far as the Conservative Party – the Whigs representing the merchant classes at the time that the Tories represented the landed classes.

Between 1867 and 1918, the Liberal Party was one of the two parties of government. By 1918, it had become the third party and its fortunes declined further over the next 30 years. In the 1970s the Liberal Party saw something of a revival and increased its share of the vote, achieving 19% of the poll in 1974. However, it then experienced another decline for several years.

After the Labour Party Annual Conference in 1980 when the left strengthened its control over the Labour Party, Shirley Williams, David Owen, William Rodgers ('the Gang of Three') and Roy Jenkins joined forces to found the *Social Democratic Party* (the SDP). Over the following months they were joined by another 30 moderate Labour MPs and a significant number of peers.

Later in 1981, the SDP and the Liberals formed *the Alliance*, remaining separate but joining forces to fight General Elections. After disappointing results from the 1983 and 1987 General Elections, David Steel (the Liberals' leader) called for the merger of the two parties, but David Owen (the SDP leader) was against that course of action. In the event, the members of both parties voted for the merger.

In 1988, a new party was formed, the *Social and Liberal Democratic Party* (SLD or the Democrats). At the end of 1989, the SLD changed its name to the *Liberal Democrats*. The SDP carried on under the leadership of David Owen with ever-decreasing fortunes, until it was wound up in 1990, by which time it had only three MPs.

The initial policy position of the party was set out in its document *Democracy of Conscience*.

For the 1997 General Election campaign, the Liberal Democrats differentiated themselves from the other two parties by being explicit about their intention to increase the rate of income tax by 1p to finance their policy options.

The Liberal Democrats – organisation and leadership

The Liberal Democrats have a federal structure, comprising three 'state' parties for England, Scotland and Wales and a federal organisation at national level.

Each 'state' party is responsible for its own organisation, finance and the selection of candidates within its 'state'.

At national level, the Federal Policy Committee looks after policy formulation and consists of the leader, the president, four MPs, one peer, three local councillors, two Scottish and two Welsh representatives and 13 other members elected by the twice-yearly Federal Conference. The FPC prepares the election manifesto in consultation with the Parliamentary party.

The Federal Policy Committee can call a ballot of the whole party on *"any fundamental question where, in its judgement, the values and objectives of the party are at issue or it is otherwise in the essential interests of the party"*.

The Federal Executive is responsible for national organisation and consists of the leader, the president, three vice-presidents, two MPs, one peer, two local councillors and 14 other members elected by the Federal Conference.

The party leader must be an MP but is elected by a ballot of all the individual members of the party – much more democratic than the other two parties.

The finance for the party is raised by membership subscriptions and fundraising at local level.

THE PARTY ORGANISATIONS – IN DIAGRAM FORM

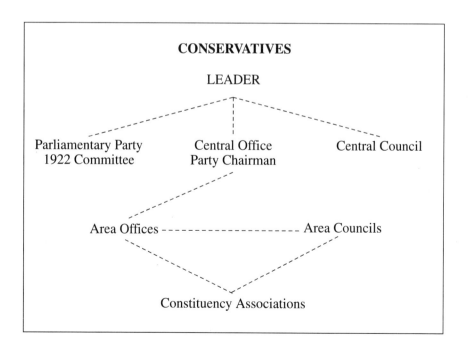

LABOUR

LEADER

Parliamentary Party

Party HQ
Party General Secretary

Annual Conference

Regional Federations — Regional Offices

Constituency Parties

Affiliated trade union
branches

Ward organisations

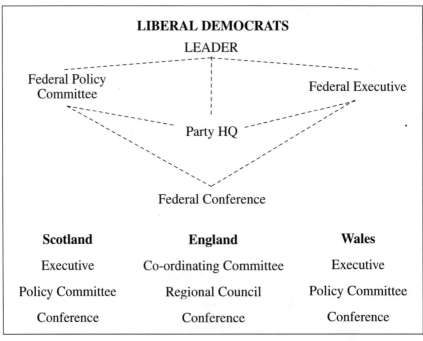

LIBERAL DEMOCRATS

LEADER

Federal Policy
Committee

Federal Executive

Party HQ

Federal Conference

Scotland	**England**	**Wales**
Executive	Co-ordinating Committee	Executive
Policy Committee	Regional Council	Policy Committee
Conference	Conference	Conference

CHAPTER 5

Elections

The Franchise – Qualifications – How elections are run – European Elections

The Franchise

The UK has universal adult suffrage – in other words, all people over the age of 18 and qualified to vote can do so. It was not always so. In 1832 at the time of the Reform Act of that year, only 5% of the adult population was entitled to vote – and they were all men. The franchise was progressively extended during the 19th century. It was not until 1928 that the UK effectively achieved universal suffrage (99%), when the vote was extended to all men and women over the age of 21 (the age of majority then).

Boundary Commissions

The UK is divided into 659 constituencies, each containing around 65,000 electors, although many constituencies will depart from this average by as much as 15,000.

Reviewing these constituencies to take account of population increase and drift is the task of four permanent Boundary Commissions, one for each of the four countries in the UK.

Each review is undertaken every 10 to 15 years and the aim is to establish approximately equal constituencies, although this is difficult to achieve in practice.

Changes which emerge from the Boundary Commission reviews can be politically sensitive, in that particular changes may favour one party or another.

Scotland and Wales have long had more seats than the size of their populations would justify – partly because they were guaranteed a minimum number of seats in the Redistribution of Seats Act 1944.

Who can vote?

UK citizens, citizens of other Commonwealth countries, and citizens of the Irish Republic resident in the UK are entitled to vote if:

- their name is on the electoral register for the constituency where they live;

- they are over the age of 18; and

- are not be disqualified from voting (as explained later).

The register is compiled annually by the local council Electoral Registration Officer. Completing the electoral registration form is compulsory, although it is not compulsory to vote. When the Poll Tax (Community Charge) was introduced by the Conservative government, many people did not have their names put on the electoral register, preferring to lose the right to vote, in an effort to avoid paying the tax.

The key date for registration is place of residence on 10 October each year. The draft register is open for public inspection until 16 December, during which period people can apply to the Registration Officer to have mistakes (usually not appearing on the register at all) corrected. After that, the register comes into effect usually on the following 16 February, although the date can change if there is a General Election.

People who are disqualified from voting are:

- peers;

- foreign nationals (including the citizens of other EU states);

- some patients detained under mental health legislation;

- convicted (but not remanded) people detained in a penal institution; and

- people convicted within the previous five years of corrupt or illegal election practices.

Members of the armed forces, Crown servants and staff of the British

Council employed overseas (and their wives/husbands if they are with them) can be registered for an address in the constituency where they would normally live. British citizens living abroad can apply to register as 'overseas electors' for a period of 20 years after they have left the UK.

Ballot papers will not be posted to an address outside the UK, so electors resident abroad (for whatever reason) necessarily have to vote by using a proxy to vote on their behalf.

Candidates

UK citizens, citizens of other Commonwealth countries, and citizens of the Irish Republic resident in the UK can stand for election as an MP, provided they are over *21* years of age and are not disqualified from sitting in the House of Commons.

Those who are disqualified from sitting in the Commons are:

- peers;

- undischarged bankrupts;

- some patients detained under mental health legislation;

- people sentenced to more than one year's imprisonment;

- clergy of the Church of England, Church of Scotland, Church of Ireland and the Roman Catholic Church;

- people personally guilty of corrupt or illegal election practices – in the last 10 years (corrupt) or seven years (illegal) if the offence was in that constituency; otherwise in the last five years (corrupt and illegal) elsewhere; and

- holders of certain offices listed in the House of Commons Disqualification Act 1975:
  — holders of politically restricted posts within the Civil Service;
  — members of the regular armed forces of the Crown or the Ulster Defence Regiment;
  — police officers;
  — holders of judicial office;
  — members of specified commissions, tribunals and other bodies (for example: Commission for Racial Equality, Lands Tribunal and Police Complaints Authority).

The election process

At least 25 days' notice of a General Election must be given. Nominations close at noon on the 19th day before the day of election (excluding Sundays and Bank Holidays). A candidate's nomination must be proposed and seconded by two 'subscribing' electors and signed by eight other 'assenting' electors – all registered within the constituency.

The nomination will also usually include a description of the candidate, of up to six words, which will appear on the ballot paper and should be sufficient to identify him or her. Although the major party candidates' descriptions are predictable, those of many of the individual candidates in 1997 were not: 'Lord Byro versus The Scallywag Tories', 'The Mongolian Barbecue Great Place to Party' and 'Space Age Superhero from Planet Beanus' were some of the more inventive and obscure!

Nominations can be withdrawn, provided this is done in writing by the candidate (with one witness) so as to reach the returning Officer by noon on the 16th day before the day of the election. A candidate does not have to be backed by a political party. The Returning Officer can refuse to accept nomination papers which appear to be out of order.

Each candidate must deposit £500 which is returned if he or she receives 5% or more of the total votes cast. The purpose behind this is to discourage frivolous candidates.

Each candidate must appoint an election agent, with an office in the constituency, to which all formal communications are sent. The maximum amount which a candidate can spend on 'election expenses' is fixed by statute – a lump sum plus an amount per elector. A candidate can post one election communication to each elector free of charge. The election agent must submit a 'return' of the candidate's election expenses not more than 35 days after the election. Failure to do so (without an 'authorised excuse' approved by a court) is an election offence, as is exceeding the statutory maximum.

Voting

People will usually vote in person at a polling station which open at 7am and close at 10pm. People who cannot reasonably be expected to vote in person (for example, away on holiday) can apply for an *absent vote* for that particular election. People who are physically incapacitated, or who cannot vote because of the nature of their work or because they have moved to a new area, can apply for an *indefinite absent vote*.

People entitled to an absent vote can either vote themselves by post or have someone else (their proxy) vote at the polling station on their behalf. Postal ballot papers cannot be sent to addresses outside the UK.

The ballot papers are issued to voters at the polling station by the election staff, who check the name of the voter against the electoral register. At this point, some people discover that their name is not on the register and they cannot vote. The polling staff are supposed to impress an *official mark* on each ballot paper before giving it to the voter, to guard against a voter introducing fake ballot papers.

At the close of the poll the ballot boxes are sealed and then taken to the counting place where they are counted either straight away or on the next day. The Returning Officer supervises the count and although the count is not open to the public, the candidates, their agents and a small number of scrutineers appointed by them can observe the count.

It is at this point that problems can arise – especially if the Returning Officer decides to disallow some ballot papers because they are spoilt or because they do not bear the official mark. Ballot papers are spoilt if the voter has put more than a cross on the ballot paper and this could lead to the voter being identified; or if the voter's intentions are unclear.

If the winner's margin is very small, the candidates can demand a recount (and more than one) until the Returning Officer decides that a demand for a further recount is unreasonable. If there is a dead heat, after recounts, then the result is decided by the drawing of lots.

If the result is particularly close, the disallowed ballot papers (if they had been allowed) might have produced a different result, and any candidate who is dissatisfied with the conduct of the election can apply to the High Court for an *Election Petition* against the Returning Officer. In the 1997 General Election, Gerry Malone lost his seat at Winchester by two votes and immediately launched an election petition to have the result overturned.

First past the post

The system in the UK involves the candidate with the most votes winning the seat – runners-up count for nothing. This is called the *'first past the post'* system and it will always lead to the result that the number of seats won by a party will not match its share of the vote. This is illustrated by the 1997 General Election results which are outlined below.

These figures demonstrate two features of the 'first past the post' system in the UK: the New Labour government may have an overwhelming number of seats, but it has less than half of the total votes cast in the UK. The substantial number of Conservative voters in Scotland and Wales have no MPs representing their point of view in Parliament.

England

	votes %	seats	seats %
Conservative	34	165	31.3
Labour	44	329	62.3
Liberal Democrat	18	34	6.4

Scotland

	votes %	seats	seats %
Conservative	18	0	0
Labour	46	56	77.8
Liberal Democrat	13	10	13.9
Nationalist	22	6	8.3

Wales

	votes %	seats	seats %
Conservative	20	0	0
Labour	55	34	85.0
Liberal Democrat	12	2	5.0
Nationalist	10	4	10.0

Proportional representation

The essential feature of a proportional representation system is that it produces a close correlation between the distribution of votes between the parties and the allocation of seats. There are various types of proportional representation systems.

The *alternative vote system* is used in Australia. Each elector puts the candidates in order of preference; the votes of those at the bottom of the poll are transferred until one candidate has half of the total vote – that candidate is elected.

The *list system* is used extensively in western Europe. Electors vote for political parties and those parties maintain national lists of their candidates. Seats are allocated to candidates from those lists in proportion to the percentage of votes secured by each party. This system produces the most proportional result, but there is no direct connection between the member and the constituency

The *additional member system* was used in West Germany. A proportion of MPs is elected in single member constituencies as in the UK. The difference comes from partial use of the list system – a second vote from regional party lists which are used to produce a degree of proportionality between the votes and MPs.

The *supplementary vote system* involves voters marking their first and second choices. A candidate who obtains over 50% of the vote is immediately elected. If that does not occur, all but the top two candidates are eliminated and second choices reallocated to produce a result.

The *single transferable vote system* is used in Ireland for large constituencies which may contain four or five members. Each elector numbers the candidates in order of preference. The minimum number of votes needed to win is regarded as a quota. Once a candidate has achieved the quota, any surplus votes for him or her are transferred to other candidates following the voters' second and lower preferences.

First past the post versus proportional representation

Criticisms of the first past the post system include:

- the government often has a majority of the seats for a minority of the votes;

- large parts of the electorate are denied representation by an MP of their political persuasion and their vote is effectively wasted;

- the large number of safe seats for the incumbent party means there is less genuine choice;

- the change in government can bring abrupt changes and frequent reversals in policy; and

- as the main parties become more regionally based as between the north and the south and as between urban and rural areas, they may become less national in their policy approaches.

Criticisms of the proportional representation system include:

- voters will be less able to hold a government responsible for its record by turning it out at the next election;

- coalition government will be less stable;

- the policy of the coalition will be a series of compromises and will lack any sure sense of direction; and

- some unsatisfactory members of the ousted coalition will reappear again in the new coalition.

European elections

The European Parliament is directly elected by the member countries. In all countries apart from the UK, some sort of proportional representation is used. Elections of Members of the European Parliament (MEPs) are held every five years – the last occasion being 1994.

There are 626 MEPs, allocated to member countries as follows:

Germany	99
UK, France and Italy	87 each
Spain	64
Netherlands	31
Portugal, Belgium and Greece	25 each
Sweden	22
Austria	21
Denmark and Finland	16 each
Ireland	15
Luxembourg	6

The Boundary Commissions produce the MEP constituencies. MEP constituencies consist of groupings of whole UK Parliament constituencies. Each MEP constituency has to be as near as possible to the 'electoral quota' – the total relevant electorate divided by the number of seats (roughly equivalent to eight House of Commons constituencies grouped together).

The European election process in the UK is broadly similar to that for the UK Parliament – but there are some differences. Unlike the UK Parliament elections, peers can vote. Peers, ministers of religion and UK MPs can stand for election as MEPs. The candidate deposit is £600, rather than £500. Nominations have to be signed by 28, rather than eight, assenting electors.

New Labour has promised a form of proportional representation, using regional lists, for the 1999 MEP elections in the UK.

CHAPTER 6

Europe

The development of the European Union – Maastricht – the single market – economic and monetary union – the EU institutions, budget and funds – other 'European' organisations

The development of the European Union

Within a space of 30 years, Europe had been the centre of two World Wars, with all the disruption such events entailed; something had to be done at the political level to prevent that ever happening again. After the Second World War it was also necessary for the heavy industries of Germany and France to be reconstructed in a way which would not threaten peace and which would ultimately lead to Franco-German reconciliation. This was the basis for the *Schuman Plan* produced in 1950, which proposed the *European Coal and Steel Community* (ECSC).

The Schuman Plan was adopted by six states: France, West Germany, Italy, Luxembourg, the Netherlands and Belgium in 1952 when ECSC was set up. Although there were some set-backs in the 1950s, this supranational approach was further developed by the Six adopting the *Treaty of Rome* in 1957, establishing two further Communities – the *European Atomic Energy Community* (Euratom) and the *European Economic Community* (EEC).

The Treaty of Rome provided for the harmonious development of economic activity, a continuous and balanced economic expansion and an accelerated rise in the standard of living. These aims were to be achieved by: the creation of a common internal market; the elimination of tariffs between member states; free movement of goods, people services and capital; and the elimination of distortions in the operation of the market.

The attitude of the UK towards Europe at this time was ambivalent, if not decidedly cool. Although the Treaty of Rome was probably seen as an interesting development, the UK believed that its main interests still lay in what was then seen as its 'special relationship' with the USA (whatever that actually meant in practice) and in the Commonwealth (which was at least growing, as the British Empire dwindled).

By 1961 it was clear that the European Communities were helping the member states to turn in strong economic performance, so four other states (the UK under Harold MacMillan, Denmark, Ireland and Norway) applied for membership. These applications coincided with the period of office of Charles de Gaulle as President of France and he effectively blocked the entry of the UK in 1963 and later, in 1967 (under Harold Wilson). Opinions differ about the reason for this hostility by de Gaulle towards UK membership, but fear of a still relatively powerful and influential rival for France within the EC seems to feature in most of them.

Although de Gaulle also appeared to be antipathetic to supranational institutions, it was possible to make some progress during the 1960s in implementing some of the EEC Treaty, including the establishment of the *Common Agricultural Policy* (CAP) and the removal of trade tariffs between the member countries.

Matters came to a head in 1965/66 when de Gaulle refused to send representatives to take part in ministerial meetings of the three Communities – the so-called 'empty chairs' crisis. This had important consequences because the solution to the problem was the 1966 *Luxembourg Compromise*, which was an informal agreement that, whatever the Treaties might say about majority decision-making, agreements between governments would be made only by unanimity or consensus. The implication underlying the Luxembourg Compromise is still important – at least for the UK, if not for some of the other members.

In 1967 the three Communities, ECSC, Euratom and EEC, were merged and became collectively known as the *European Community* (EC).

The first increase in the EC came in 1973 when the UK (under Edward Heath), Ireland and Denmark joined the Six. By this time, de Gaulle had been replaced by Georges Pompidou. The 1970s saw little in the way of further progress in integration, apart from the establishment of the *European Monetary System* (EMS) in 1979.

There followed two further enlargements: in 1981 Greece joined; and Spain and Portugal acceded in 1986.

A more significant development, in terms of supranational integration, came with the *Single European Act* (SEA) taking effect in 1987. The SEA was the first comprehensive revision of the original 1957 treaties, confirming their aims and objectives. Further integration was promoted in two ways: the speeding-up of economic integration; and the strengthening of the supranational institutions to speed-up the decision-making process. The enthusiasm generated by the SEA in turn led to pushing on with other earlier ideas for integration, such as *European Monetary Union* (EMU) which had been under discussion for some years.

The reunification of Germany, in October 1990, effectively added the former democratic republic of East Germany to the EC.

The most recent treaty revision exercise took place at the end of 1991 and led to the new all-embracing Treaty on European Union (popularly known as the *Maastricht Treaty*, from the name of the Dutch city where it was signed). However, this time, the process was not entirely smooth.

The Maastricht Treaty provisions had to be ratified at national level and there were difficulties in this in two countries, Denmark and the UK. Was this due to the supranational policy-making élite being out of touch with the true wishes of the people of the nation states, who viewed further integration with some suspicion – especially given the uncertainty about some fundamental questions in Europe?

The first Danish referendum in June 1992 was against ratification and this was seen as a threat to the whole process, until the second Danish referendum in May 1993 supported ratification. But the Danish experience had the knock-on effect of prolonging the process of ratification by a UK Parliament which was reluctant to cede sovereignty to the EU ('the European Super State' was one of the pejorative terms used by Mrs Thatcher while she was Prime Minister).

The UK eventually ratified the Maastricht Treaty, but only after securing the *Social Protocol*. This Protocol enabled the UK to opt out of the extension of EU social policy (usually called 'the Social Chapter') into areas of UK economic activity over which the then UK Conservative government preferred to retain national control. These opt-out provisions might be viewed as repeating the safeguards of the informal 1966 Luxembourg Compromise and they reflected continuing unease in the UK Parliament about the sovereignty issue.

By a further treaty signed at Corfu in June 1994, Austria, Finland and Sweden joined the EU in 1995. The Corfu Treaty also envisaged the accession of Norway, but they decided not to join.

A number of the emerging democracies in central and eastern Europe have applied to join and have agreements with the EU which may lead to membership. The EU itself has agreed to start accession negotiations with Cyprus and Malta six months after the present Intergovernmental Conference has finished.

The UK's New Labour Government has indicated, in its first Queen's Speech in May 1997, that it will 'opt into the Social Chapter'.

The Maastricht Treaty

This treaty eventually came into effect in November 1993 after ratification by the member states. The treaty had various effects:

- introduced new commitments, moving toward economic and monetary union (EMU) in three stages, the third stage being a single European currency;

- established the *European Union* (EU) from a combination of the European Community (EC) and the intergovernmental arrangements for a common foreign and security policy *(see the later section Decision-making in the EU);*

- set up the framework for a *Common Foreign and Security Policy* (CFSP) with its own Secretariat, under which intergovernmental decisions were to be taken only on a unanimous basis;

- increased co-operation on interior/justice policy issues;

- codified the principle of *subsidiarity* (action should be taken at European level *only* if its objectives cannot be achieved by member states acting *alone* and can be better achieved by the Community – a principle which is of particular importance to the UK, reluctant to see the centralisation of power in Brussels, but which is also important for other member countries which view the principle as authorising devolution of power to regional level within member states); and

- introduced the concept of European Union citizenship, supplementing national citizenship.

The Maastricht Treaty has some other implications which are mentioned in the sections which follow.

Maastricht is not the end. In March 1996 an Intergovernmental Conference

(IGC) was convened by EU heads of government to consider further treaty amendments. The European Council Summit met at Amsterdam in late June 1997 to consider how to convert the IGC conclusions into a further treaty.

The Single Market

The single market provides for the free movement of people, goods, services and capital, as envisaged by the Treaty of Rome in 1957.

This is achieved by removing customs tariffs, liberalising the movement of capital, opening up public procurement to all member states and the mutual recognition of professional qualifications. The object of all of this is to reduce business costs and increase efficiency, widen consumer choice and create jobs and wealth.

The first stage of European Economic and Monetary Union (EMU) as envisaged by the Maastricht Treaty was the completion of the single market by 31 December 1993. By the *European Economic Area* (EEA) *Agreement*, which came into force on 1 January 1994, most of the EU single market provisions were extended to Iceland, Norway and Liechtenstein.

That is the theory. In practice, individual countries can find ways of inhibiting trade between member states, often to protect domestic industries. Germany used its strict brewing laws, at least for a time, to prevent the sale of 'poor quality' UK beer in Germany.

Following the BSE outbreak in the UK, the export of UK beef to other EU countries was banned on grounds of 'public health' – probably, it has to be said, understandably at the time. By June 1997 the UK government believed, on the basis of expert technical advice, that its slaughtering and animal health arrangements had become the best in the EU.

The UK government was disappointed that the ban on UK beef imports to other EU countries had not been lifted, despite requests for this to happen. It therefore felt justified in threatening to ban the import into the UK of beef from those EU countries with 'inferior' arrangements, on 'public health' grounds. Banning such imports for 'tit-for-tat' or purely trade reasons would have contravened the EU treaties. Not quite the free movement of goods!

European Economic and Monetary Union (EMU)

This is likely to be one of the major issues facing the EU in the next few years. Given the reasons for the original foundation of the EC/EU, it is hardly surprising that the idea of monetary union has been on the agenda for many years – at least since the 1970s.

A start was made by establishing a currency unit (the European Currency Unit or 'ecu') which is used only for internal EU purposes.

The EMU was originally due to have been achieved by 1980, at least in theory. However, the programme was effectively stopped by a combination of the 1973 oil crisis and the wild fluctuations in the international monetary system which that crisis caused.

In 1979, another attempt was made, but this time it was more modest – the European Monetary System (EMS). A component of EMS was the *Exchange Rate Mechanism* (ERM) which the UK did not initially join, because it was felt at that time that membership of ERM would inhibit UK domestic economic policy.

However, by October 1990 the then Chancellor of the Exchequer, John Major, was able to persuade Mrs Thatcher that it would be a good idea for the UK to join the ERM. The UK was forced to withdraw from the ERM in September 1992 ('Black Wednesday') after Norman Lamont, the then Chancellor of the Exchequer, had spent a phenomenal amount of the UK's reserves in trying (and failing) to maintain the value of the Pound within the ERM limits, in the face of determined currency speculation. The Italians also had to withdraw the Lira from the ERM at the same time.

The ERM experience goes a long way towards explaining the UK's subsequent scepticism about EMU, which was the objective then envisaged by the Maastricht Treaty.

The Maastricht Treaty envisaged progress towards full EMU in three stages:

- *Stage 1:* Concluded at the end of 1993 with the practical completion of most of the single market;

- *Stage 2:* Began on 1 January 1994, with the establishment of an advisory and consultative *European Monetary Institute*; monetary policy remains with national governments who co-ordinate their economic policies within agreed, but non-binding, guidelines; and

- *Stage 3:* A single currency, the *'Euro'*, planned for completion by 1 January 1999, but problems are already starting to appear.

The UK negotiated a special Protocol (an 'opt-out') to the Maastricht Treaty which recognised that the UK was not obliged to move from Stage 2 to Stage 3 of EMU.

Those member states who wish to move to Stage 3 have to satisfy certain *convergence criteria* on inflation rates, government deficits, currency fluctuation margins and interest rates – and those convergence criteria are the source of some of the problems. The governments of Germany and France have so far expressed complete confidence that they will achieve Stage 3 by the Maastricht deadline. However, the economic measures that they have been obliged to impose on their people in order to meet the EMU inflation and public deficit criteria are not very popular amongst their electorate.

The government of Germany encountered difficulty in June 1997 when it attempted to revalue (upwards) its gold reserves – its independent Central Bank, the Bundesbank, accused the Bonn government of creative accountancy in order to improve Germany's chances of meeting the government deficit criterion.

The people of France decided, in June 1997, to elect a socialist government, as the people of the UK had done the previous month. However, there was one important difference – the brand of socialism in France was not the same as New Labour's; it was old-fashioned socialism, promising large-scale creation of employment presumably through increased public expenditure. The implications of this for France's chances of meeting the government deficit criterion are as yet unclear.

It is now being said, by EMU supporters, that the Maastricht convergence criteria are not as fixed as everyone believed them to be and are capable of more 'flexible' interpretation – presumably to keep alive hopes that the Maastricht deadline for the first wave of countries adopting the *Euro* can still be achieved.

The European institutions

The main European institutions are:

- The European Commission

- The Council of Ministers

- The European Council

- The European Parliament (EP)

- The European Court of Justice (ECJ).

There are others: *the Court of Auditors* which monitors EU expenditure; the *Economic and Social Committee* which is consulted on legislation and is one of the routes by which special interest and pressure groups are able to make their views known; and the *Committee of the Regions* established under the Maastricht Treaty as a means of involving the regions in those EU policy areas with geographical aspects.

Issues of national pride would suggest that a single location was not an achievable objective anyway, but one of the aspects which tends to make the EU seem rather remote from the ordinary people is the location of its various institutions. The European Commission is based in Brussels. The EP has its plenary sessions in Strasbourg, its committee meetings in Brussels, and its Secretariat based in Luxembourg – the logistics must be horrendous. The ECJ is based in Luxembourg.

The European Commission

Put simplistically, this is, in effect, the EU Civil Service – but it is far more than that. Unlike national equivalent organisations, the Commission can initiate policy, proposing legislation without waiting for instructions or guidance from ministers. The Commission carries out the decisions of the Council of Ministers and checks that EU rules are observed by the member states. The Commission can also develop ideas which transcend national interests – sometimes described as being 'the conscience of the European Community' – but it must be sensible if they are to survive the legislative process.

The Commission is organised into Directorates-General, the equivalent of Whitehall ministries, and each policy area is overseen by one of 20 Commissioners (one per member state, except for the five most populous, UK, France, Germany, Italy and Spain, which have two each). One of the Commissioners acts as President of the Commission.

The Commissioners are expected to support the interests of the EU rather than their own nation states. Their period of office is, as a result of the Maastricht Treaty, now five years to synchronise with the EP electoral cycle, and their appointment is subject to EP approval.

The Council of Ministers

The Council of Ministers is the main decision-making body of the EU. It comprises the ministers of the 15 member states, representing the subjects under discussion, so its precise membership (and name) will vary according to the subject-matter being discussed; for example 'the Council of Agriculture Ministers' will include the UK Minister for Agriculture, Fisheries and Food and 'the Council of Economic and Finance Ministers' will include the UK Chancellor of the Exchequer. The Council has met in about 20 different guises and will have included ministers from all UK ministries except Defence.

The main task of the Council of Ministers is to take policy decisions which are political in nature and its work is supported by the *Committee of Permanent Representatives* (COREPER). Like the Council, the precise membership of COREPER will vary according to the subject matter under discussion – and will consist of permanent civil servants from each member state, or each member state's ambassador to the EU.

The President of the Union is responsible for chairing all meetings of the Council of Ministers and COREPER, and holds office for six months, on a rotational basis between the member states. The UK will next hold the Presidency in the first half of 1998. Because of the relatively short period of office (six months is hardly long enough to learn the ropes), the Secretariat of the Council provides a large degree of continuity, in much the same way as the UK Civil Service.

A distinctive feature is the system of voting – by weighted majority voting. The size of each member state's weighted vote is approximately proportional to its population, so UK, France, Germany and Italy each have 10 votes, Luxembourg has two and the rest have a number in between. Where qualified majority voting is in operation, significantly more than a bare majority is required.

The total number of votes is 87 at present and a blocking minority is at least 26 votes. This will change when the EU is next enlarged – but the 1997 *Amsterdam Summit* failed to agree on what the changes should be.

What this means is that, in theory, the UK can sometimes be outvoted and be expected to implement the legislation agreed by the majority. Little use was made of the feature until the SEA and Maastricht. However, it is still not as simple as the treaties might suggest – only consensual policy stands the best chance of implementation throughout the EU.

The European Council

The European Council was established in 1974 and comprises the member states' heads of government (France sends its President), their foreign ministers and two Commissioners (the President and one other). The more important meetings, especially if treaty modification is on the agenda, tend to be called 'Summits'. Of all the EU institutions, the Council is probably the best placed to initiate major policy developments, if only because of its composition.

The European Council meets at least twice each year in the final month of each Presidency, hosted by the country just concluding its Presidency. The Council can be something of a media event, with little real outcome. However, it has some significant policy developments to its name; for example: the SEA, EMU and Maastricht.

The European Parliament (EP)

The EP was originally known as the *European Assembly*. Its current membership is 626 directly-elected MEPs, of which the UK has 87. The UK (except Northern Ireland) MEPs are elected by the 'first past the post' system – the remainder are elected by some form of proportional representation.

The EP is there to be consulted about major decisions and now shares power with the Council over the EU budget. It is interesting to see how the powers of the EP have developed.

The EP was first directly elected in 1979 and had fairly limited powers. At that time these were confined to giving non-binding opinions on proposed EC legislation; the right to examine the work of the Commission and the Council; and the ability to dissolve the Commission (which it never exercised).

However, the rôle of the EP was enhanced when it gained some influence over the EC (now EU) budget. The EP could, by an absolute majority, block the EU budget, but has only dome so once – in December 1979. The SEA introduced some further development by giving the EP a part to play in the legislative process in certain policy areas – the 'Co-operation Procedure' – and thus enabled it to influence the Council in those areas.

This process of developing the power and influence of the EP was taken one step further by Maastricht, by introducing a new power of 'Co-decision' – put simply, this new power can enable the EP to reject legislation, rather than comment upon it. Rejection requires an absolute majority – an example being the rejection of Commission proposals to ban 'Superbikes'. Much of EU legislation now goes through either the co-operation or co-decision procedure and the EP's detailed work is done in its committee system.

However, the EP still has nothing like the legislative powers of its member state counterparts and perhaps it would be a little naïve to expect otherwise. Certainly, its split-site arrangements mentioned earlier do not help it to operate as effectively as it might. The difficulty facing the EP is also compounded by its internal politics, within which there are, necessarily, transnational political groupings – with members with ostensibly similar political ideologies (but from markedly different national political traditions) having to learn to live with their internal differences. Still, it is the only example of its kind in the world!

The European Court of Justice (ECJ)

Each member state provides one judge to sit on the ECJ, whose rôle is to interpret the EU treaties and EU law. The 15 judges are assisted by nine Advocates-General. The work of the ECJ is assisted by a *Court of First Instance*, which deals with certain types of cases brought by companies and individuals.

The importance of the ECJ should not be underestimated – not least as a vehicle for UK constitutional change. The body of EU law and treaty provisions is increasing, as is its impact on the citizens of the member states and the rights which they enjoy.

The important point is that EU law now has precedence over domestic UK law and its implementation within the UK can be enforced by the ECJ. For example, in the field of employment law, ECJ decisions on the legal effect of the EU *Acquired Rights Directive* changed fundamentally the way in which the UK's Transfer of Undertakings (Employment Protection) Regulations (TUPE) were implemented in the UK. The ECJ decision meant that the employment rights of *public* sector employees were protected to the same extent as those of private sector employees – thus putting a large dent in the Conservative government's plans to privatise public services.

The nature of EU law is also important – its terminology is necessarily general because it needs to make some sort of sense for all of the different internal arrangements within the 15 member states. So, this broad-brush approach enables the ECJ, in interpreting what EU law actually means, to *make* law to a greater extent than any of its national counterparts.

Decision-making in the EU

Put simply, proposals usually originate from the Commission, which by then will have consulted interested parties and groups, often through the extensive lobbying arrangements which exist at EU, as well as national, level.

Proposals from the Commission are sent to the Council of Ministers and are usually looked at first by COREPER, on behalf of the Council. At the same time the proposals are also sent to the EP and the Economic and Social Committee, each of which makes its views known to the Council.

Finally, the Council will reach a decision (taking into account the advice it has received from the EP and the Economic and Social Committee), using whatever voting method is relevant for the particular policy area involved.

However, there are important areas of policy which are deliberately *not* handled through the mechanisms set out in the treaties. This approach started in 1970 with foreign policy but has since been extended to police co-operation, drug-smuggling, cross-border crime and immigration. For these particular issues, member governments have wanted to retain an element of national sovereignty, preferring to deal with them at inter-government level – effectively keeping them out of the hands of the Commission and the EP; and largely out of the public arena.

The Maastricht Treaty to some extent gave formal authority to this inter-governmental activity by recognising it as providing, with the EC, two of the three components of the EU. One was the Common Foreign and Security Policy (CFSP) and the other was *Judicial and Home Affairs* (JHA) co-operation. Decisions within these two components are, unlike the other EU treaty-based arrangements, unanimous only – so national sovereignty in these areas of policy is preserved. There is no accountability to the EU institutions – information, only, is supplied.

The product of the decision-making process emerges from the Commission or the Council of Ministers in different ways. *Regulations* are of general application and are, in effect, EU law, binding as such. *Directives* are also of general application and are binding, but only in relation to the objective to be achieved, leaving the means of doing so up to each member state within its domestic law. *Decisions* are directed towards specific bodies and are binding only on those bodies. Finally, *Recommendations* and *Opinions* can be issued – which, as their name suggests, are not binding.

The Community budget

The Community's income consists of:

- levies on agricultural imports;

- customs duties;

- proceeds of a notional rate of VAT of up to 1.4% on a standard 'basket' of goods and services; and

- contributions from member states based on their gross national product (GNP).

In the case of the UK, it has an annual rebate worth £2 billion because, without a rebate of that value, its net contribution would be much more than was justified by the UK share of the EU GNP.

The future shape of EU finance was reached at a European Council Summit in Edinburgh in 1992, because of concerns about the future size of the EU budget. The overall revenue ceiling was kept at 1.2% of EU total GNP until 1995. Since 1995, the ceiling has risen, in steps, with the aim of reaching a new limit of 1.27% of EU total GNP by the end of 1999.

By the end of 1999, Agricultural spending is planned to be less than 50% of the total budget – compared with 80% in 1973 and 60% in 1996.

The Edinburgh Summit also agreed to allocate more funding to the poorer regions of the EU.

Community Policies and Funds

The *Common Agricultural Policy* (CAP) is designed to secure food supplies and stabilise markets – it has, however led to over-production (various food 'mountains' and 'lakes') and put pressure on the EU budget. The operation of the CAP seems to excite universal criticism.

The *Common Fisheries Policy* (CFP) concerns the conservation and management of fish stocks. This is achieved by setting annual total allowable catches (TACs) for different species of fish which are then allocated to EU member states, taking account of traditional fishing patterns.

The phenomenon of *Quota hopping* has appeared whereby UK registered fishing boats are, in fact wholly or partly owned by foreign interests, but use up the UK fishing quotas and then land most of their catch outside the UK. The UK government is attempting to have the EU treaties changed at the 1997 Amsterdam Summit so that member states can exert some control over the way their fishing quotas are used.

The EU also operates a number of *Structural Funds* aimed at:

- promoting economic development in underdeveloped regions;

- regenerating regions adversely affected by industrial decline;

- combating long-term unemployment and helping young people to enter the labour market;

- helping workers to adapt to changes in industries and systems of production;

- streamlining agricultural production, processing and production systems; and

- promoting rural area development.

The *European Regional Development Fund* finances infrastructure projects and industrial investment. The *European Social Fund* supports training and employment initiatives aimed at young people and unemployed people. Agricultural restructuring is funded via the *European Agricultural Guidance and Guarantee Fund*. The modernisation of the fishing industry is supported by the *Financial Instrument of Fisheries Guidance*.

The Maastricht Treaty set up a *Cohesion Fund*, designed to reduce the differences between levels of development in richer and poorer member states – becoming more important as the EU increases in geographical size.

The *European Investment Bank* is a non-profit making institution which lends funds for public and private capital projects – concentrating on the less favoured regions, improving transport infrastructure, improving industrial competitiveness and protecting the environment.

Other 'European' bodies

So far, this chapter has been about the EU and its institutions. However, there are other institutions, some with the word 'Europe' in their name, which need to be explained, if only to distinguish them from, and avoid confusion with, the EU institutions. These further institutions may cover Europe in a wider geographical sense than that implied by the EU and may even be international and rather less formal. The more important of them feature in the remainder of this chapter.

The Council of Europe

This is *not* the same as the EU institution called the European Council.

The UK is a founding member of the Council of Europe, membership of which is open to any European democracy which accepts the Rule of Law and the protection of fundamental human rights and freedoms. At present there are 39 member states who co-operate on such matters as culture, education, health, anti-crime policy, anti-drug trafficking measures and environmental improvement.

In 1950, the Council adopted its European Convention on Human Rights (more properly called the *European Convention for the Protection of Human Rights and Fundamental Freedoms*).

The European Convention on Human Rights

The Convention seeks to guarantee and protect:

- the right to life, liberty and a fair trial;

- the right to marry and have a family;

- freedom of thought, conscience and religion;

- freedom of expression, including freedom of the press;

- freedom of peaceful assembly and association;

- the right to have a sentence reviewed by a higher tribunal; and

- the prohibition of torture and inhuman or degrading treatment.

If any individual or group believe that they have been treated in violation of the Convention, then they can complain to the *European Commission of Human Rights* in Strasbourg. Theoretically, a state can complain about the behaviour of another state, although this is seldom done.

The next step involves the Commission deciding whether the case is admissible and, if it is, trying to reach a compromise between the parties. If this process of conciliation fails, then the Commission or the state concerned can refer the case to the *European Court of Human Rights* (which sits in Strasbourg) to rule on whether or not the Convention has been breached.

Any state which is a signatory to the Convention is morally bound to change its domestic law if that law is found by the Court to be in breach of the Convention. One of the more recent examples of this process in action in the UK concerns corporal punishment in schools. A case was brought before the Court against the UK government arguing that corporal punishment in schools (which was then lawful) amounted to "inhuman or degrading treatment", contrary to the Convention. The Court agreed and the UK had to change its domestic law making corporal punishment in schools unlawful.

The New Labour Government plans to incorporate the Convention into UK domestic law, making it more directly enforceable.

There are proposals in the 11th Protocol to the Convention (signed and ratified by the UK) which envisage the replacement of the existing Commission and Court by a new full-time Court.

International conventions

While on the subject of Human Rights, it is worth just mentioning the wider context, since this is sometimes also confused with the European arrangements just described.

The *Universal Declaration of Human Rights* was adopted by the United Nations General Assembly in 1948. This was not a binding document in the strictly legal sense, so the General Assembly adopted two International Covenants; one dealing with economic, cultural and social rights, and the other covering civil and political rights. These covenants came into force in 1976 and there is a UN treaty monitoring committee which receives reports on compliance from participating states.

To complete the picture, there are other international conventions which the UK has signed, on:

- the prevention of genocide;

- torture and other cruel, inhuman or degrading treatment or punishment;

- the elimination of racial discrimination;

- the elimination of discrimination against women;

- the rights of the child;

- the status of refugees; and

- the abolition of slavery.

CHAPTER 7

The National Health Service

Administrative structure and finance

Development

The National Health Service (NHS) was created in July 1948 as part of the social welfare policies of the Labour government (under Clement Attlee) immediately after the Second World War. The social welfare policies went beyond the NHS and were aimed at providing universal and free welfare benefits for those people who were in need – *'from the cradle to the grave'*. Such an approach had been envisaged by William Beveridge's 1942 Report on *Social Insurance and Allied Services*, which provided the plan for the development of the UK's welfare state.

Since the 1940s, the original 'free of charge' approach has been significantly modified, so that many aspects of the NHS are now paid for – by those deemed able to afford to do so.

Administration at national level

The Secretary of State for Health in England and the relevant Secretaries of State for Scotland, Wales and Northern Ireland are responsible for the administration of the NHS in their areas.

The Departments supporting the Secretaries of State are:

● *England* – Department of Health

● *Scotland* – Scottish Office Department of Health

● *Wales* – Welsh Office

● *Northern Ireland* – Department of Health and Social Services.

The *NHS Executive* in the Department of Health has the rôle of developing and implementing policies for the provision of health services in England. The Executive is responsible for planning, resource allocation and major capital projects. The eight regional offices of the NHS Executive replace the 14 regional health authorities (RHA) which were abolished in April 1996.

Administration at local level

In England and Wales, prior to April 1996, the NHS was administered by District Health Authorities (DHA) which were responsible for providing hospital-based services and by Family Health Service Authorities (FHSA) which were responsible for community-based services. Their responsibilities have now been combined and given to all-purpose Health Authorities (HA) or Commissions, whose boundaries largely reflect the former DHA boundaries – covering populations ranging from 125,000 to 1 million.

The rôle of the new health authorities is not to provide services themselves, but to assess the needs of their population, produce plans and then buy in healthcare services to meet the needs identified in the plans. In Scotland, health boards carry out similar responsibilities. The HAs involve local people, local authorities, hospitals, community health services and GPs in the planning process.

Community Health Councils

In each health authority's area there are Community Health Councils (CHC) which enable local opinion to be expressed on the health authority's plans and the standard of service being provided. CHCs comprise representatives of local authorities, voluntary organisations and other people with an interest in local health services. CHCs usually produce annual reports. The equivalent to CHCs in Scotland are Local Health Councils.

NHS Trusts

The NHS and Community Care Act 1990 introduced the idea of NHS Trusts. A hospital or health service unit (for example, an ambulance service or a community health service) could apply to become a 'self-governing' NHS Trust, independent of direct local health authority control. Similar arrangements were introduced in Northern Ireland for Health and Social Services Trusts, which have more responsibilities because of the greater integration of health and social services there.

Trusts are still part of the NHS, accountable to the relevant Secretary of State and have to produce business plans, annual reports and accounts, and hold at least one public meeting each year. A board of directors runs the

Trust, which can employ staff, set its own pay and conditions, carry out medical research and even treat private patients. By the middle of 1996 there were over 520 NHS Trusts.

NHS Trusts derive most of their income from providing services under contracts with health authorities and GP fundholders.

GP fundholders

As a result of the 1990 Act, in England and Northern Ireland, GP practices with more than 5,000 patients are eligible to apply for 'fundholder status'. When the scheme was first introduced, the threshold was 11,000 patients. The threshold was progressively reduced to broaden the scheme. By April 1996, 52% of the English population were registered with 3,700 fundholding GP practices. In Wales and Scotland, the present threshold is 4,000 patients.

The object of this scheme is to give GPs the opportunity to manage a proportion of the NHS budget allocated to them, leading (it is said) to better management and control of costs and innovative methods of patient care. The budget is used to buy non-urgent hospital services from any hospital in the UK, public or private. Community nursing services can be bought from the NHS and the budget covers the charges for the cost of drugs issued on prescription by the practice and the costs of running the practice itself.

The NHS internal market

In the previous sections 'purchasing' and 'providing' healthcare services have been mentioned. On the face of it, the NHS is not an obvious choice for an internal market approach (even one which is planned and regulated), given that it is tax-financed and largely free of charge at the point of delivery.

The 1990 Act introduced the concept of an internal market (involving a so-called 'purchaser/provider split') following a 1989 White Paper *Working for Patients*. The rationale was that the introduction of competition would lead to the attainment of the '3 Es' – efficiency, effectiveness and economy.

The main purchasers in the NHS are the HAs and fundholding GP practices. The main providers are NHS Trusts and suppliers of secondary healthcare, such as dentists, opticians and chiropodists.

When the internal market was first introduced, the approach to contracting was cautious – fairly simple fixed-price block contracts confirming the present supply arrangements, to minimise disruption. As the participants (especially the purchasers) gained experience, so the nature of the contracts changed – to more closely specified but still fixed-price contracts or variable-price contracts linked to volume or the complexity of individual cases.

There have been problems with NHS Trusts and the internal market. Some of the smaller Trusts rapidly realised that they were not viable and had to be taken over by larger Trusts, presumably to gain from economies of scale. Mergers brought with them 'rationalisations' of hospital facilities – including the closure of complete hospitals or A&E departments, provoking much, but largely ineffectual, public outcry.

The operation of the NHS internal market has led to a burgeoning bureaucracy within the NHS, especially in managing the more complex variable-price forms of contract. This has diverted resources away from clinical and nursing services.

The Audit Commission has been critical of what it sees as the relatively low '3 Es' gain by GP fundholders from the internal market so far. The New Labour Government may introduce changes in the way fundholding GP practices contract with providers, in order to simplify the system.

The operation of the internal market has produced variable quality of performance and market-driven short-term financial considerations, which have had an adverse effect on the concept of 'equity' in the NHS – that is, fair and consistent access to NHS services across the whole of the country. The government's reoccupation with demonstrating the benefits of the internal market for reducing waiting lists for certain kinds of surgery led, it is said, to a skewing of surgical services so that waiting lists for other kinds of surgery lengthened.

How the NHS is funded

Just over 80% of NHS expenditure is met through general taxation. The remaining 20% comes from:

- the NHS element of National Insurance contributions;

- charges to patients for drugs and treatment;

- income from land sales and income generation schemes; and

- funds raised from voluntary sources.

In 1995/96 NHS gross expenditure amounted to £33,400 million.

NHS and PFI

The NHS Trust process was seen as one of the ways of encouraging private sector participation in capital development in the public sector – through the Private Finance Initiative (PFI). The government made much of its scheme to promote the design, construction and operation of new hospitals through PFI.

Although many schemes were approved (50 since 1992), the programme effectively stalled due to the complexity of the negotiations. There were also doubts within the private sector financiers about whether the NHS Trusts had the necessary legal power to enter into PFI agreements at all – without that power, the agreements would be unenforceable.

The New Labour Government clearly regards PFI as the best way of improving the NHS infrastructure, given the limitations on public expenditure which it has accepted. It has taken two courses of action to get the programme going again – the responsibility for pushing schemes forward has been transferred from NHS Trusts to the NHS Executive; and legislation has been promised, removing any doubts about the legal powers of NHS Trusts to complete PFI agreements.

Health Service Commissioners

There are three Health Service Commissioners (one each for England, Scotland and Wales). In practice, the three posts are held by one person who is generally called 'the Health Service Ombudsman' and who is also Parliamentary Commissioner for Administration (the Parliamentary Ombudsman). In Northern Ireland, the Commissioner for Complaints undertakes a similar rôle.

The Commissioner handles complaints made by members of the public that they have suffered injustice or hardship as a result of:

- failure in service from an NHS body;

- failure to provide a service which the person was entitled to receive; or

- maladministration by an NHS body.

The Commissioner produces an annual report for Parliament.

In 1996, the scheme was extended to cover complaints in respect of all family health service practitioners and about the exercise of clinical judgment.

Patient's Charter

The Patient's Charter is an extension of the Citizen's Charter programme. The aim of the Charter is to describe the rights of patients and the standard of service which they can expect to receive from the NHS. Each of the four countries in the UK has its own Patient's Charter.

The first English Patient's Charter came into force in 1992 and was extended in 1995 to cover dental, optical and pharmaceutical services as well as the hospital environment. The standards of service cover:

- respect for the individual patient;

- ambulance waiting time;

- A&E clinical assessment;

- out-patient clinic appointments; and

- cancellation of operations.

In addition, there are separate charters on maternity services (1994), blood donation (1995) and hospital and community services for children and young people (1996).

NHS Trusts and GP practices are also encouraged to produce their own charter covering the standards of the services which they provide.

Openness in the NHS

Another aspect of a quality service is the provision of appropriate information. The NHS Code of Practice on Openness came into force in 1995. The Code applies to NHS Trusts, health authorities and local health practitioners (GPs, dentists and pharmacists).

The Code describes the information which should be published or made available about:

- the services provided, their cost and effectiveness and the performance targets set and results achieved;

- proposed changes in health policies or the way services will be delivered; and

- access to one's own health records.

CHAPTER 8

Social Welfare Services

Administrative structure and benefit system

Administration

The present system of social welfare services also has its roots in the 1942 Beveridge Report. The main government department overseeing the system is the Department of Social Security (DSS), although the day-to-day work is carried out for the DSS by a number of executive agencies, including an agency from another government department.

The executive agencies are:

- *Benefits Agency* (BA) – administers and delivers most benefits;

- *Child Support Agency* (CSA) – assesses and collects maintenance payments for children;

- *Contributions Agency* – collects National Insurance contributions;

- *Information Technology Services Agency* – computerises social security administration;

- *War Pensions Agency* – services to war pensioners; and

- *Employment Services Agency* (DfEE) – pays benefit (Jobseeker's Allowance) to unemployed people on behalf of the Benefits Agency.

The *Housing Benefit* and *Council Tax Benefit* schemes are run by local authorities which recover most, but not all, of the cost from the government.

The CSA has the dubious distinction of having alienated practically everybody with whom it has had contact. The agency was beset with administrative problems right from the start and failed to meet the performance targets set for it. To improve its chances of meeting its targets, it concentrated on the 'easy' absent fathers, leaving the 'difficult' ones for later.

The single mothers saw no real advantage from the payments extracted from absent fathers, because these were used to offset the cost of benefit payments made to the mothers. Indeed some suffered hardship – the CSA was so inefficient that mothers often found their benefits quickly reduced by the more efficient BA, with the CSA failing to make up the shortfall by collecting the absent father's assessed contribution on time.

Even some of the absent fathers had cause for complaint – when the CSA assessed them for payments, even though they had earlier reached what they thought was a 'clean break' divorce settlement, often approved by the court. In some cases, the additional unlooked-for payments threatened the stability of the father's second family.

The future of the CSA is under review by the New Labour Government – which consistently criticised the CSA when in opposition.

Social security benefits – summary

There are three main types of social security benefit:

- *contributory benefits* – available to people with a satisfactory history of payments into the National Insurance Fund;

- *income-related benefits* – available to those people whose income falls below a specified threshold; and

- *other benefits* – available to those people who satisfy specified tests – for example, disability or family needs.

Social Security is the largest public expenditure programme – planned expenditure for 1996/97 was £76,800 million, almost one-third of the total. The relative size of the benefit programmes can be judged from the fact that contributory benefits take up about one-half of the expenditure, income-related benefits almost one-third and other benefits about one-sixth.

As far as funding for the social security programme is concerned, general taxation provides a half, employers' NI contributions about a quarter and employees' NI contributions about one-fifth.

The whole social security benefit system is complex and only the more significant types of benefit are described later in this chapter. The New Labour Government has committed itself to a fundamental review of the state benefit system. Since most of them are changed annually in line with inflation, no rates are given. Some benefits are tax-free; others are taxed. The types of benefit currently available (and the current rates and conditions) can be checked in the helpful booklets produced by the DSS.

National Insurance (NI)

The *National Insurance Fund* is a statutory fund which receives all NI contributions from employers, employees and self-employed people and meets expenditure on contributory benefits.

There are five classes of NI contributions:

- *Class 1:* Paid by both employers and employees, where employees are paid above a specific threshold. An *employee's* contributions are based on a percentage of his or her pay up to a specified upper limit. The *employer's* contributions are also based on a (higher) percentage of the employee's pay and there is no specified upper limit. The contribution can be lower if the employer operates a 'contracted-out' occupational pension scheme;

- *Class 1A:* Paid by an employer who provides the benefit of a car and/or fuel to an employee, for private use. The amount is related to the cash equivalent of the benefit provided;

- *Class 2:* Paid by self-employed people earning above a specific threshold. Paid at a flat rate per week. See Class 4;

- *Class 3:* Paid voluntarily to safeguard one's rights to some benefits. Paid at a flat rate per week;

- *Class 4:* Paid by self-employed people in addition to Class 2 contributions if their taxable profits exceed a specified lower threshold. Based on a percentage of those profits up to a specified upper limit.

Employees who work after reaching pensionable age (women at 60 and men at 65 as the law presently stands) do not pay NI contributions, but the employer does. Self-employed people over pensionable age do not pay NI contributions.

Contributory benefits

These benefits are available only if NI contributions have been paid. The individual concerned must have paid a minimum number of contributions to obtain any benefit at all; and the amount of benefit depends on the number of contributions actually paid. Many people receive less than the maximum benefit.

There are five contribution-based benefits, supplementing the statutory maternity and sick pay schemes:

- *Retirement Pension:* This is payable to women at the age of 60 and to men at the age of 65. The Sex Discrimination Act 1986 does not prevent the different treatment of men and women within the state pension scheme. Retirement ages for men and women will be equalised (to 65), the change being phased in over 10 years from April 2010. Women born before April 1950 will still retire at 60; those born after April 1955 will retire at 65; those born in between 1950 and 1959 will retire between 60 and 65 according to their year of birth.

- *Widows' Benefit:* This is payable to widows under the age of 60 or to widows over that age whose husbands were not entitled to a state pension when they died.

- *Statutory Sick Pay/Incapacity Benefit:* Statutory Sick Pay is payable by employers from the fourth day of sickness for up to 28 weeks, a single rate, to those employees earning more than a specified threshold. Incapacity Benefit is payable when any Statutory Sick Pay paid by an employer ceases or to those who do not qualify for Statutory Sick Pay at all. There are three rates of benefit which vary according to the period of the incapacity. New more stringent tests have been introduced to ensure that only those people incapacitated for any type of work will receive this benefit after an initial period.

- *Statutory Maternity Pay?Maternity Allowance:* Statutory Maternity Pay is payable (for up to 18 weeks) by employers to women who have worked for that employer

114

for a specified minimum period and paid above a specified threshold. Maternity Allowance is payable (also for up to 18 weeks) to women who are not eligible to receive Statutory Maternity Pay from their employer or who are self-employed.

- *Jobseeker's Allowance:* This was introduced in October 1996 to replace unemployment benefit and income support for unemployed people. There are two types of Jobseeker's Allowance: contribution-based and income-based; both paid by the DfEE Employment Services Agency on behalf of the DSS. The contribution-based allowance is payable for up to six months and is not means-tested. The income-based allowance is payable to those on low income and is means-tested, taking into account family circumstances and commitments.

Income-related benefits

These are paid to people whose family income falls below a specified threshold and are means-tested, particularly in relation to any savings or capital. The application of a means-test will often result in no benefit being payable. The one exception to this is Child Benefit, which is not means-tested and is paid regardless of income.

- *Income Support:* This is payable to people who are not expected to be available for work: lone parents, pensioners, carers and long-term sick and disabled people. The amount received depends upon family income (including other social security benefits), savings and commitments. This used to be available to unemployed people on low incomes, but was replaced in October 1996 by the income-related Jobseeker's Allowance.

- *Housing Benefit:* This is payable, by local housing authorities on behalf of the DSS, to people having difficulty paying their rent. The amount received is calculated taking into account factors similar to those for Income Support. In relation to private sector tenants, benefit is based not on the actual rent paid but on average rents for property of that size in the area – to encourage people to move to more cost-effective accommodation.

- *Council Tax Benefit:* This is available to people having difficulty paying their council tax and is awarded by the local authority responsible for collecting council tax allowing a percentage rebate (up to 100%) on the council tax bill. The amount of the rebate is calculated taking into account factors similar to those for Income Support.

- *Family Credit:* This is paid to low-income employed and self-employed working families with children, with the objective of encouraging them to stay in work. The amount depends upon the family net income and the number and ages of dependent children within the family.

- *Earnings Top-up:* This was introduced in October 1996 on a pilot basis in eight areas only and is, in effect, equivalent to Family Credit (with the same objective), but for single people or couples without children. This new benefit may be abandoned or extended nationally, after a review of its effectiveness.

- *Child Benefit:* This is not means-tested, is the main benefit for children and is normally paid to the mother. The amount depends upon the number of children in the family and is paid for children up to the age of 16, or 19 if the child is in full-time non-advanced education.

The Social Fund

This fund covers a range of additional benefits, most of which are means-tested and, therefore, may not be paid. The benefits are payable to people receiving some of the income-related benefits described in the last section and entitlement varies. In one case (the discretionary crisis loan) receipt of another income-related benefit is not required to qualify.

The main point is that the Social Fund consists of two types of payment: *regulated* and *discretionary*. There is no financial limit on the regulated payments, but the discretionary payments come out of a capped part of the Social Fund (£141.5 million for 1996/97) and when the money runs out, that's it.

Regulated payments are:

- *maternity payment:* a lump sum for each baby born or adopted;

- *funeral payment:* a lump sum to meet specified expenses; and

- *cold weather payment:* a weekly payment towards heating costs in very cold weather from November to March, payable only to those on Income Support who are elderly, disabled or have children under the age of five years.

Discretionary payments are:

- *community care grant:* to help people remain in the community, or resettle into the community after a period in care;

- *budgeting loans:* for important intermittent expenses; and

- *crisis loans:* for help in an emergency or disaster where there is a serious risk to health or safety.

Other benefits

As mentioned earlier, there are other benefits which are payable to people who satisfy specific tests other than income, for example disability.

- *Severe Disablement Allowance:* This is payable to people who are not eligible to receive Incapacity Benefit because they have a poor NI contribution record. Claims can be made by people aged between 16 and 65, but is payable beyond the 65th birthday. There are stringent medical tests.

- *Disability Living Allowance:* This is payable to people who became severely disabled before the age of 65 who have personal care needs or who need assistance with mobility. The allowance has two components: care and mobility. The amount depends upon the level of attention they need. People who are terminally ill receive a higher amount.

- *Attendance Allowance:* This is payable to people severely disabled on or after their 65th birthday and is similar to the Disability Living Allowance, although the amounts are different.

- *Invalid Care Allowance:* This is payable to people between 16 and 65 years old who cannot take on a paid job because they are caring for someone who is receiving the middle or higher rate of the care component of the Disability Living Allowance.

- *Disability Working Allowance:* This is payable to people who are aged 16 or over; who are working at least 16 hours per week on average; but who have an illness or disability which puts them at a disadvantage in getting a job. The allowance is means-tested and income-related and is only paid if the applicant qualifies. To qualify, the applicant must be receiving the Disability Living Allowance (or an analogous benefit under the war pensions or industrial injuries schemes); or have an invalid three-wheeler or other vehicle under the NHS Act 1977; or have received one of several specified benefits but at their higher rates.

New Labour's 'New Deal' – 'Welfare to Work'

As part of the July 1997 Budget Statement, Gordon Brown announced that the benefits system would be modified so as to encourage young people and single parent mothers to enter or return to the workplace – 'Welfare to Work'.

As far as young people were concerned, there would be a package of measures aimed at encouraging them to enter work or training and offering financial incentives to employers to take on unemployed people. For young people, staying at home and doing nothing on State benefit would not be an option – indeed, benefit would be stopped for a short period if the young person was thought to be dragging his or her feet in pursuit of training or work. The basic problem, however, remains – providing training that is relevant and there being a worthwhile job available at the end of the training.

As far as single-parent mothers were concerned, the key change would be in the amount of their wages which working mothers were allowed to keep (the 'disregard') before their benefit was reduced – to cover the cost to them of arranging day-time childcare to enable them to go out to work. In this case, the real problem is the apparent shortage of nursery and child-minding places needed to support the proposed expansion in the number of mothers in employment.

Reviews and appeals

By now the complexity of the scheme, if not much else, will be clear. The entitlement rules are complex and will be applied by thousands of individual officers in the various executive agencies. Mistakes will be made and there needs to be a system through which incorrect or unfair decisions can be reviewed and challenged.

Not all decisions made by or on behalf of the DSS are susceptible to appeal – for example, a decision made about a Social Fund *discretionary* payment can only be *reviewed* by the Social Fund officer who made it; that is as far as the process goes.

Some of the appeal mechanisms are limited – either on the grounds upon which an appeal can be lodged or the time within which it can be made – for example appeals on Disability Living Allowance (DLA), Disability Working Allowance (DWA) and Attendance Allowance (AA) decisions. There are different procedures for handling CSA and war pension appeals.

The process usually starts with the original decision of an Adjudicating Officer or the Adjudicating Medical Authority about entitlement to benefit or the amount to be paid or the medical condition of the applicant. People are encouraged to try to settle the matter locally, without going to formal appeal, by asking for their case to be looked at again – a *review*.

If the claimant remains dissatisfied after the review, then he or she can proceed to *appeal*, if there is the right to do so. In each case, the appeal tribunal is independent of the DSS, but it can only apply the existing DSS regulations; it cannot make new rules. There are three tribunals and the one actually used depends upon the particular benefit in dispute.

The *Social Security Appeal Tribunal* (SSAT) hears appeals about all Adjudication Officer decisions, except those about disability. The SSAT has a legally qualified chairman and two other people.

The *Disability Appeal Tribunal* (DAT) hears appeals about DLA, DWA or AA decisions made by an Adjudicating Officer. The DAT has a legally qualified chairman and two other people – one of whom is a doctor (usually a GP) and the other is someone who knows about dealing with the needs of disabled people.

The *Medical Appeal Tribunal* (MAT) hears appeals about decisions made by an Adjudicating Medical Authority. The MAT has a legally qualified chairman and two other people, both of whom are doctors who are consultants.

The appellant will be asked whether an oral hearing is needed or whether the appeal can be decided on the basis of the documents which the appellant has submitted (a 'paper hearing'). The appellant does not need to attend an oral hearing but is encouraged by the DSS to do so: *"please note that claimants who attend the hearing of their appeal usually do better than those who do not"*. People appealing to the MAT will usually be expected to attend, since the consultant doctor members of the tribunal will want to make their own medical examination.

The tribunal phase of the appeal process is not the end. It is possible to take an appeal one stage further – to a *Social Security Commissioner* – but only on a point of law, not on a point of fact or on a medical issue. The Social Security Commissioner is a lawyer who is independent of the DSS, the Employment Service agency of the DfEE and the tribunals. Both sides, the appellant and the Adjudication Officer, may appeal to a Commissioner.

CHAPTER 9

Employment and Training

The promotion of industry and employment – helping unemployed people find work

Promoting industry and employment

The economic health of the UK depends upon a variety of factors, the more important of which are industrial activity and the employment of people. Apart from issues of self-esteem, people who are in work do not generally require social security benefits, so reducing public expenditure and the need for additional taxation. Therefore, an important part of government policy is the encouragement of new industry (especially to replace old industries) within the UK to improve its trading position in the world.

This encouragement takes two forms: the improvement of the physical industrial plant and environment to meet modern standards and to create or retain jobs; and the improvement in the training of the potential workforce so that its skills match those currently required by industry. Some of the training schemes have had varying degrees of success – often young people go through a training course (including work experience) only to find no suitable work waiting for them at the end. Because of this, the range of training initiatives is continually changing in the search for greater success.

The final stage is helping people to find those jobs which are available and suited to the skills which the people have acquired through training. Each of these will be considered in turn.

Job creation through regeneration

The next few sections deal with the various government schemes (some with EU assistance) which, over a period of years, have been aimed at improving and regenerating the industrial infrastructure. Most of these schemes have been under the auspices of the DoE, although in recent years there has been greater emphasis on using the integrated Government Offices for the Regions.

Urban Development Corporations

Originally there were 122 Urban Development Corporations (UDCs)to tackle large-scale urban decline. Three (Bristol, Leeds and Central Manchester) have been wound up. The remainder (London Docklands, Merseyside, Birmingham Heartlands, Black Country, Plymouth, Sheffield, Trafford Park, Teesside, and Tyne and Wear) are due to be wound up by March 1998.

Public expenditure by UDAc in 1996/97 was £208 million, including the London Docklands Light Railway.

Enterprise zones

Twenty-eight enterprise zones have been created, the first of which was established in 1981. Each zone has a life of 10 years, so most have ceased to exist. There seems to be no intention to extend the enterprise zone arrangement generally, but it may be used exceptionally if there is a large-scale loss of jobs in a particular area. The zones were intended to generate private sector interest in the area to create jobs and encourage redevelopment.

The facilities available in an enterprise zone are: exemption from national non-domestic rates; 100% corporation and income tax allowances for new industrial and commercial development; and a simplified land-use planning system.

Task Forces

These are intended to have a limited existence – the aim is to deal with the problem and strengthen local organisations which can then take over future management. Task Forces are small teams (about five or six people) from government departments, local authorities and the private and voluntary sectors.

The objective is the economic regeneration of specific inner-city areas with an emphasis on improving local employment and training opportunities. Since the first Task Forces came into existence in 1986 a total of £148 million has been spent under the programme, helping to provide over 37,000 jobs and 17,000 training places.

English Partnerships

This is a government regeneration agency which concentrates on the development of vacant, derelict or contaminated land. As its name suggests, the agency works in partnership with other public bodies and the private and voluntary sectors. The objective is to stimulate local enterprise, create jobs and improve the environment.

In 1994/95, 250 projects were approved, creating 13,200 jobs and reclaiming 4,000 acres of land. The planned gross expenditure under this programme in 1996/97 is about £207 million and the programme is itself eligible for help from the European Regional Development Fund.

The *Rural Development Commission* undertakes a similar rôle in the countryside where problems of social and economic decline are often as acute as those in urban areas. The Commission plans to spend £44 million in 1996/97, largely through the 312 *Rural Development Areas.*

City Challenge

The City Challenge initiative was started in 1991 – local authorities were asked to submit bids in partnership with the private and voluntary sectors, local communities and government agencies. The objective was to deal with problems of physical decay, lack of economic opportunity and poor quality of life in key neighbourhoods within the local authority area. The financial objective was to use government funding to attract a larger amount of private finance. In the six-year period to 1997/98 the government hopes that the £1,163 million of City Challenge funding will have attracted over £3,500 million of private sector investment.

Single Regeneration Budget

The Single Regeneration Budget (SRB) came into existence in 1994/95, bringing together 20 programmes from five government departments – including those mentioned in the previous four sections. The idea of combining resources to deal with regeneration problems had been piloted under the City Challenge initiative and was found to be successful.

The main programmes funded through the SRB are administered by the integrated Government Offices for the Regions, combining the previous regional offices of the DoE, DfEE, DTI and DoT. The SRB allocation for 1996/97 was £1,318 million.

Wales

In 1994 a new *Strategic Development Scheme* (SDS) was established, taking over the previous Urban Programme. The budget for 1996/97 was £63 million, generating more than £80 million of private investment.

Urban Investment Grants (1996/97 budget – £6.8 million) are used to encourage private sector investment in derelict and run-down sites in urban areas.

The *Welsh Development Agency* (WDA) aims to promote industrial efficiency and improve the environment. Its land reclamation programme is the largest and most sustained in Europe (£314 million spent so far to bring 6,500 hectares back into productive use). Its capital development programmes (£850 million spent in the last 20 years) provide readily available industrial premises. The WDA claims to have created over 90,000 new jobs and saved 50,000 existing jobs.

Development is also encouraged by the *Land Authority for Wales,* a self-financing statutory body which ploughs back its profits into further schemes. The aim is to assemble land for development where the private sector would find it difficult to do so.

The first *Programme for the Valleys* (1988-93) was a scheme for the economic and physical regeneration of the South Welsh valleys, co-ordinating the activities of the WDA and other public and private sector bodies. This has been followed by a second five year programme (1993-98) with broader objectives to do with housing, health, training and job-creation.

The *Cardiff Bay Development Corporation* was set up in 1987 to revitalise the south part of Cardiff. The Cardiff Bay barrage scheme will, when completed, create a large freshwater lake, although there have been concerns about its environmental impact. The Development Corporation's aim is the creation of 25,000 new jobs and the construction of 6,000 new homes.

Scotland

There have been initiatives in Scotland similar to those in England, the most notable being a partnership approach, using *Urban Programme* funding (the Urban Programme funding disappeared into the SRB in England), on which detailed decisions are taken by the local partnership. The comprehensive regeneration strategy has been based on the experience gained from four Partnerships – Dundee, Edinburgh, Glasgow and Paisley – which were set up by the Scottish Office in 1988.

Scottish Enterprise (the Lowlands) and *Highlands and Islands Enterprise* (the Highlands) are two bodies which manage government and EU support to industry and commerce. They aim to attract inward investment and encourage new businesses, as well as improve the environment by reclaiming derelict and contaminated land.

Northern Ireland

Job creation and improvement in the environment in Northern Ireland is achieved through the *Urban Development Grant*, which is directed towards the partnership schemes in the inner-city areas of Belfast ('Making Belfast Work') and Londonderry ('Londonderry Initiative').

The smaller towns are covered by the *Community Regeneration and Improvement Special Programme* which is jointly funded by the Department for the Environment for Northern Ireland and the *International Fund for Ireland*, established by the UK and Irish governments in 1986, whose donors include the US, EU, Canada and New Zealand.

Industrial development and international investment in Northern Ireland is promoted by a combination of the *Industrial Development Board, the Local Enterprise Development Unit* and the *Training and Employment Agency.*

Regional Grants

There are some parts of the UK where additional help with economic growth and enterprise is thought to be necessary. These are identified as *Assisted Areas (Development Areas* and *Intermediate Areas)* and cover about 35% of the UK working population. Some areas are identified as having been adversely affected by colliery closures or the decline in the shipbuilding industry.

Inward investment into these areas, especially to create jobs, is encouraged by a system of grants: *Regional Selective Assistance, Regional Investment Grants* and *Regional Innovation Grants*. The grants are administered by the Government Offices for the Regions, the Scottish Office Industry Department and the Welsh Office Industry and Training Department.

EU Programmes

The EU structural funds and their purpose have been described in the chapter on Europe. The *European Social Fund* supports training and employment initiatives aimed at young people and unemployed people

The most relevant of the EU structural funds for regeneration is the *European Regional Development Fund* (ERDF) – particularly for areas affected by industrial decline. The DoE co-ordinates the ERDF programmes in England and during the period 1994-96 £1,195 million had been allocated from the ERDF.

Merseyside is now regarded as an area which merits 'Objective 1' support (promoting economic development in underdeveloped regions), which is the highest level of Structural Fund support. Between 1994 and 1999, Merseyside is due to receive £633 million on this basis.

In addition to Merseyside, there are six 'non-Objective 1' urban areas in England which will receive funding under the *URBAN Community Initiative,* which is an EU-wide (rather than regional) scheme aimed at promoting urban regeneration in a way which complements the relevant domestic programmes.

Job creation through training

The other way in which people can be helped to gain employment is to ensure that they are trained in skills which are marketable and which industry needs. The government department most involved in the training aspect is the Department for Education and Employment (DfEE) and its aims are achieved through a variety of mechanisms and bodies – in many cases involving the employer side of industry, local chambers of commerce, employers' organisations and the Confederation of British Industry (CBI).

The employer side of industry and commerce

Chambers of commerce are locally-based organisations established to promote the economic development of local businesses and are a focal point for the exchange of information and ideas at local level.

Employers' organisations usually exist on an industry basis – for example the Engineering Employers' Federation – and although they may have interests in pay-bargaining and industrial relations, they also have interest in training within the relevant industry.

Trade associations tend to consist of businesses which produce a specific product or specific range of products. They aim to provide support services to, and act as spokesman for, their members.

The *Institute of Directors* (IOD) provides business advisory services to its 35,000 company director members, many of whom run small businesses.

The *Confederation of British Industry* (CBI) is an influential national organisation which represents, directly or indirectly 250,000 businesses. It is the largest organisation of its type in the UK and many chambers of commerce, employers' organisations and trade associations are in membership.

The CBI has 12 regional offices and an office in Brussels. It offers its members a forum where issues can be debated, a lobby for influencing government and a range of support services.

Training and Enterprise Councils (TEC) and
Local Enterprise Companies (LEC)

Training and Enterprise Councils (TEC) are quangos which exist in England and Wales as independent companies with employer-led boards. There are 81 TECs, of which seven merged with local chambers of commerce to become 'Chambers of Commerce, Training and Enterprise'.

TECs are an important instrument of government training policy. They manage the provision of training and enterprise programmes for several government departments under contracts which are supervised by the Government Offices for the Regions. The programmes are diverse and the range of providers under TEC contract include most further education colleges – with the result that TECs now control the supply of virtually all work-related further education.

The DfEE training programme delivered through TECs amounted to £1,200 million in 1996/97. The DTI provides funds to TECs to deliver its enterprise programmes. Many of the projects funded through the Single Regeneration Budget (SRB) have a TEC as their lead organisation.

In Scotland, the equivalent organisations are the 22 *Local Enterprise Companies* (LEC) which are supervised by Scottish Enterprise and Highland and Islands Enterprise. The LEC rôle is both wider and narrower than that of a TEC: LECs have responsibilities for economic development and environmental improvement, but have no responsibilities for work-related further education.

Industry Training Organisations (ITO)

Industry Training Organisations exist to deal with training issues (including ensuring that needs are met and standards maintained) for a particular sector of industry, commerce or the public service. They have a rôle to play in developing occupational standards and NVQs and their Scottish equivalent. By September 1997, ITOs will be replaced by a national network of National Training Organisations.

National Targets for Education and Training

This was an initiative set up by the CBI in 1991 and is supported by the government, TECs, LECs and ITOs. The aim is to improve the UK's international competitiveness by raising training and attainment levels in education and training. The Targets cover both young people ('Foundation Learning Targets') and the whole workforce ('Lifetime Learning Targets').

Training for Work

This is a government programme aimed at helping unemployed and disadvantaged adults to find work through a combination of training and work experience. People between 18 and 65 years of age, who have been out of work for six months or longer, receive an individually-tailored programme of training and/or work experience.

As an incentive to join the programme, participants receive a premium payment on top of their normal benefit. The planned budget for 1996/97 is £485 million and the programme is provided through contracts managed by TECs and LECs.

Investors in People

TECs and LECs provide information and advice to the organisations which participate in the Investors in People Scheme. The scheme aims, through the application of rigorous standards, to improve the performance of organisations by linking the training and development of all employees with the achievement of specific business objectives.

About 25,000 organisations employing more than 5 million people have agreed to participate in the scheme – the incentive to do so is that the Investors in People logo indicates a quality organisation and is good for business!

Modern Apprenticeships, National Traineeships and Youth Credits

These are government initiatives to improve the range of training available to young people, so that every young person, who is not in full-time education or who does not have a job, can be offered a suitable training opportunity.

Modern Apprenticeships came into full operation in 1995, after pilot schemes had been run in some areas, covering over 50 industrial sectors. Over the last 10 years or so, traditional apprenticeships on offer had rapidly declined and these Modern Apprenticeships are seen as a means of reversing that trend and producing a supply of young people trained to technician, supervisor or equivalent level – up to NVQ level 3.

National Traineeships are planned to come into existence in September 1997. They are intended to train young people to NVQ levels 1 and 2, through a "broad and flexible learning programme", including skills in communication, numeracy and information technology.

Youth Credits are available to all 16 and 17 year old school and college leavers and are intended to enable young people to have more individual choice in training and "a greater sense of personal responsibility" when buying their training. The Youth Credits are like Education Vouchers – presented to employers and training providers in return for training. The equivalent scheme in Scotland is *Skillseekers*.

Finding work

Once opportunities for work have been created and people have been trained, work has to be found for them. This is the task of the Employment Services Agency (the Employment Service) of the DfEE.

The Employment Service runs about 1,100 local offices (*Jobcentres*) where people can see details of job opportunities and be interviewed and offered advice. The Jobcentres also operate the Jobseeker's Allowance scheme on behalf of the Benefits Agency of the DSS. The Employment Service works under a *Jobseeker's Charter* which defines the level of service which unemployed people can expect to receive, both in terms of advice and the payment of benefit.

When a newly unemployed person arrives at a Jobcentre, he or she is interviewed by a *New Client Adviser*. The interview not only checks entitlement to benefit, it also results in a *'Back to Work Plan'* which is a description, agreed with the client, of what steps (including the type of work) the client will take to find work or training.

If the person is still unemployed after 13 weeks, then he or she will be interviewed again, this time in more depth, with the aim of broadening the type of work (beyond his or her normal occupation) which the person will consider. The Back to Work Plan is regularly reviewed, since one of the performance targets set for the Employment Service is a specific percentage reduction in the number of unemployed people.

In addition to advice at Jobcentres, the Employment Service runs a variety of programmes:

- *'1-2-1'* – intensive help with looking for work, for those who have been unemployed for more than one year; 239,000 places offered in 1996/97;

- *Jobplan* – guidance to those unemployed for more than one year in assessing their skills, qualities and training needs;

- *Jobclubs* – training and advice on job-hunting and access to facilities to help a more intensive job search;

- *Restart courses* – rebuilding self-confidence and motivation and help with job-finding skills; and

- *Work trials* – encouraging employers to take on for a short period (three weeks) people who have been unemployed for more than six months, to assess their potential.

Specialist services are available for people with disabilities, who have access to *Disability Employment Advisers* in Jobcentres. The specialist advisers are part of integrated teams – *Placing Assessment and Counselling Teams*. The specialist services include:

- *Access to Work* – helping young people with disabilities to overcome barriers to employment; and

- *Supported Employment Programme* – providing opportunities to some 21,800 people with severe disabilities whose productivity levels would make it difficult for them to keep a job in an open placement – similar to a sheltered employment scheme where specific employers receive payments to compensate them for the low productivity of their disabled employees.

CHAPTER 10

Industry and Commerce

Industrial relations – health and safety – forms of corporate organisation – the London Stock Exchange – competition

Industrial relations

Industry will operate more efficiently if there are arrangements in place for maintaining good industrial relations between the two sides: employers and the workforce. Industrial relations include not only collective bargaining but also the settlement of collective disputes and ensuring a safe working environment.

Industrial relations is in essence a voluntary process, affected in some respects by the forces of the marketplace: shortage of labour possessing the required skills; shortage of jobs. However, over time, successive governments have underlined the importance of good industrial relations by intervening and putting in place a degree of regulation on both sides and a means by which the resolution of disputes can be helped.

The employer side is regulated by the health and safety legislation and the employee side is regulated by the progressive limitation on the ability of trade unions to strike. The resolution of disputes is helped by the government's Arbitration, Conciliation and Advisory Service (ACAS).

Trade unions – the national scene

In the previous chapter on *Employment and Training*, mention was made of the employer side of industry and the representative organisations fulfilling that rôle. The employee side has also evolved its own means of representation – the trade unions.

It is often forgotten that for many years before the turn of this century, trade unions were illegal – 'combinations' of labour were outlawed by successive Acts of Parliament. As this century progressed, with the advent of Labour governments, trade unions became more powerful and the previous statutory limitations on their freedom of action were eliminated. With the advent of the Thatcher Conservative government, the pendulum started to swing back again (but not as far) as limitations were reimposed on the ability of trade unions to disrupt industry through strike action.

Trade unions are not just about pay and conditions bargaining – they will aim to provide their members with benefits and services, including educational and social facilities, and legal and financial advice.

Over the last few years, the overall picture on trade unions has been changing. The total number of trade union members nationally has declined and the proportion of male trade union members has also declined. This has been put down to two main factors: the shift in the scope of industry away from manufacturing to service industries, where unionisation is less prevalent; and the shift in the nature of work from full-time to part-time, in which women are more prevalent.

At the end of 1994, there were 8.3 million people in trade unions, the lowest figure since 1945. The number of trade unions has declined by about one-third over the last 20 years – mostly by mergers. The most recent merger produced the largest trade union (1.4 million members), UNISON, from three public sector unions: COHSE, NALGO and NUPE. Three other unions have over 500,000 members: T&GWU, GMB and AE&EU.

There is now a *Certification Officer* whose job is to certify the independence of individual trade unions. 'Independence' means a union which is truly independent of the employer and thus more likely to represent the interests of its members fearlessly, rather than a fairly weak staff association which is dependent upon the employer.

The Certification Officer also lists the employers' organisations.

Trade unions – the local scene

Although the internal organisation of trade unions varies, there will usually be a national executive committee and there may be a regional or district organisation, if the union is large enough to need it.

Unions usually have to be 'recognised' by the employer for collective-bargaining purposes and once recognition is granted, a work place organisation will be set up by the union to handle formal relations at that level.

A union will have a branch organisation which may cover more than one work place. Where an employer has recognised more than one union for the same workplace, there is usually a 'shop stewards' committee' to iron out any differences. 'Shop stewards' are workplace representatives elected at local level and should be distinguished from the full-time paid officials of the union.

Trades Union Congress

Most (but not all) trade unions are affiliated to a national organisation called the *Trades Union Congress* (TUC). Note the title: the old-fashioned plural of 'trade union' was 'trades union'. The TUC was founded in 1868 and its affiliated membership (1997) consists of 71 trade unions, representing 6.75 million people or 80% of trade union members nationally.

The aims of the TUC are to promote the interests of its affiliated organisations and to improve the economic and social conditions of working people generally. The questions it deals with tend to be broad ones, affecting trade unions generally, both in the UK and internationally. The TUC is itself affiliated to international labour organisations: the *International Confederation of Free Trade Unions* and the *European Trade Union Confederation*.

Apart from holding its own annual Congress each September, the TUC nominates the British workers' delegation to the *International Labour Conference*.

The TUC has six regional councils in England and a single one for Wales – the Wales Trades Union Council. There is a body equivalent to the TUC in Scotland: the *Scottish Trades Union Congress*. In Northern Ireland, the trade unions there are represented on the *Northern Ireland Committee* of the *Irish Congress of Trade Unions* (ICTU).

Industrial action – trade union immunities

As mentioned earlier, some statutory limitations have been imposed on the ability of trade unions to call upon their members to take strike action whenever they want.

Strike action by an employee amounts to an unlawful breach of contract, upon which the employer can act – either by firing the employee or by suing for damages. Industrial action falling short of strike action may or may not amount to breach of contract.

When a trade union instructs its members to take strike action, the union is inciting breach of contract and can also, in theory, be sued for damages by an employer. In many cases, employers will be more interested in getting their employees back to productive activity than in starting theoretical legal proceedings, but the important point is that employers can go to court to obtain injunctions if unions are acting unlawfully – a much more effective weapon.

However, trade unions can claim immunity from legal action, but only in specific circumstances. The most important point is that the industrial action must be *"wholly or mainly in contemplation or furtherance of a trade dispute"* between workers and *their own employer*. Striking about something unrelated to a trade dispute (for example, the company's activities in another country) is unlawful. Striking about another company's employees is also unlawful.

It is also unlawful for trade unions to involve workers who have no dispute with their own employer – *'Secondary picketing'* – to limit the spread of the industrial action. There is also a limit on the number of picketers who may be placed outside a work place – to avoid 'intimidation' of those workers not in sympathy with the dispute.

The union also has to go through the correct procedure before the industrial action can proceed – any mistakes and the industrial action is unlawful. The process involves a secret postal ballot of its members to obtain support for the proposed action (the union can reclaim from the government the costs incurred in the postal ballot) and it must tell the employer of the holding of the ballot. If the ballot authorises industrial action, then the union must give the employer at least seven days' written notice of the intended action and the details of the ballot result.

Advisory, Conciliation and Arbitration Service

The *Advisory, Conciliation and Arbitration Service* (ACAS) is a quango appointed by the DTI but independent of it, with the rôle of promoting the improvement of industrial relations in the UK except Northern Ireland. In Northern Ireland the analogous body is the *Labour Relations Agency*.

The title of ACAS indicates its various functions:

- *advice* – aimed at preventing industrial action in the first place; often general advice developed jointly with employers' and employees' organisations – sometimes in the form of Codes of Practice;

- *conciliation* – intervenes in a dispute when invited to do so; the process of conciliation involves mediation in the dispute, but the product of the mediation is *not* binding on the parties; and

- *arbitration* – intervenes in a dispute when invited to do so; the process of arbitration involves mediation in the dispute, and the product of the mediation *is* binding on the parties.

ACAS also has a rôle in individual, as opposed to collective, disputes. Whenever anyone starts an action in an industrial tribunal (unfair dismissal, sex or racial discrimination), an ACAS Conciliation Officer will be assigned to try to broker a binding settlement between the parties.

Health and safety

Industry will be more productive if there is a safe working environment and this is sufficiently important to have been made the subject of stringent statutory regulation – the main provision being the *Health and Safety at Work etc. Act 1974.*

The duties imposed by the 1974 Act itself affect everyone alike – employers, employees, self-employed and manufacturers and suppliers of work equipment. The 1974 Act has a series of subordinate statutory instruments or regulations, the more notable of which is the *Control of Substances Hazardous to Health Regulations 1988* (revised 1994). The 1988 Regulations constitute a systematic and comprehensive set of measures controlling exposure to virtually all of the substances known to be hazardous to health.

The *Health and Safety Commission* (HSC) has the job of developing policy on health and safety matters, including simplifying the statutory regulation regime. Its work is supported by a number of advisory committees; for example toxic substances, genetic modification and nuclear installation safety. There are also advisory committees dealing with specific sectors of industry.

The *Health and Safety Executive* (HSE) is the body responsible for enforcing health and safety legislation. The day-to-day work is carried out by the *Field Operations Division,* incorporating the Factory, Agricultural and Quarries inspectorates, together with regional staff from the *Employment Medical Advisory Service.* The current issue is the relatively small number of inspectors for the job in hand.

The enforcement of some health and safety legislation is the responsibility of local authorities – offices, shops, warehouses, restaurants and hotels – working under HSE general guidance.

In Northern Ireland there is a broadly similar system. The *Health and Safety Agency* is roughly equivalent to the HSC; enforcement is, however, split between the inspectorates of the *Department of Economic Development* and the *Department of Agriculture*.

The commercial context for industry

Industry does not operate in a vacuum. The aim of industry is to provide employment for people and to make profits for the benefit of the company and its shareholders and, indirectly, for the benefit of the UK economy as a whole. If the industrial and commercial base of the UK is strong, so will be its place in the world economic scene.

The economy can be thought of as consisting of two sectors: the public sector (which covers all government-related activity, usually funded through taxation, public loans and gilt-edged securities and bonds) and the private sector (which covers activity by private – i.e. non-government – companies, bodies and individuals, usually through private resources, private loans or capital raised through the sale of shares and other securities).

There is an increasing trend for government to use companies from the private sector to finance, wholly or partly, major public capital works and then manage them, in return for an annual payment from the government – for example, the Private Finance Initiative (PFI). The financing of the controversial Skye Bridge and some new motorways are examples of the way the private sector is used to improve the infrastructure of the country without increasing the public sector borrowing requirement.

There are various forms of company corporate structure and the economic health of UK companies is reflected through the London Stock Market.

Corporate structures – limiting liability

A person who carries on business on his or her own account, does so at considerable personal financial risk. The individual is personally responsible for all the debts and liabilities of the business. The same is true if a group of people join together to run a business – a partnership. In the case of a partnership, each partner is jointly and severally liable with all the other partners for the whole business.

There will come a point in any business (including at the outset) where the decision is taken to limit the personal liability of the people running the business – and this is achieved by adopting a corporate form of organisation – a limited liability company.

There are three broad types of limited liability company: a company limited by *guarantee;* a company limited by *shares*; and a *public* limited company (plc).

A *company limited by guarantee* is the form of organisation usually adopted by non-commercial organisations, such as theatre trusts. There is no share capital; instead, the liability of individuals is limited to the amount (usually £1) which the 'subscribers' agreed, when they signed the company's original memorandum and articles of association. A company's memorandum and articles of association are, in effect, its constitution, including a description of its powers and objects.

A *company limited by shares* is the form usually adopted by small to medium sized businesses, especially those in private hands. The personal liability of the owners of the business is limited to the nominal value of the issued share capital. In the very smallest companies very few shares will have been issued and these will be retained by the original owners or their immediate family.

A *public limited company* (plc) is similar to a company limited by shares, but with one important difference – the company's operations will be very much larger and it will need to raise a larger amount of capital in order to fund its operations and development. That capital is raised by the plc selling its shares to members of the public and, if appropriate, those shares are traded on the London Stock Exchange.

London Stock Exchange

The main administrative base of the London Stock Exchange is in London, with regional offices in Belfast, Birmingham, Glasgow, Leeds and Manchester. The Exchange has moved away from traditional floor-based trading to screen-based trading.

There are about 2,600 UK and overseas companies listed on the Exchange with a combined capital value of £3,370,000 million. Their shares ('equities') are traded in the Exchange. A new computerised settlement system for shares and other securities, CREST, will eventually eliminate the need for share certificates – towards a paperless Exchange.

The advent of screen-based trading has enabled the performance of the securities traded on the Exchange to be judged almost every second, although hourly and daily price movements are usually reported. The usual measures of the prices of shares traded on the Exchange are the series of *FTSE Actuaries Share Indices*. There are nine indices, the most popular being the *FTSE 100* (the share prices of the 100 largest UK companies) and the *FTSE All-Share*. The abbreviations 'FT-SE' and 'Footsie' are registered trade marks of the Financial Times/London Stock Exchange!

Competition

An economy will work for the benefit of consumers if there is genuine competition, keeping prices down. Although the Conservative government was keen on deregulation of the market place, there were limits.

Any true monopoly will be in a position to charge what it likes for its goods and services. A small number of suppliers may not constitute a monopoly but may still be able to control prices by forming a cartel. Either of these situations is undesirable and there are mechanisms to prevent them, if they work against the public interest.

Overall competition policy is the responsibility of the *Department of Trade and Industry* (DTI) under the President of the Board of Trade. Competition law is administered by the *Director General of Fair Trading*, the *Monopolies and Mergers Commission* and the *Restrictive Practices Court*. Apart from UK competition law, there is also the added dimension of EU rules, enforced by the EU Commission.

In UK competition law terms, a *monopoly* is where a single business supplies or purchases at least 25% of a particular product or service. A *complex monopoly* is where a group of companies jointly have 25% of the market or where they behave in a way which affects competition in the market place.

Sometimes *mergers* of companies could result in a monopoly situation and merger proposals are closely examined. Either the Director General or the President of the Board of Trade can refer a proposed merger to the Monopolies and Mergers Commission (MMC) for detailed examination.

The MMC investigation will either approve the merger (there may be a monopoly, but it is not one against the public interest), or reject it, or require *undertakings* to be given before it can proceed. For example, when brewery companies propose to merge, quite often they have to give undertakings to restructure their businesses and dispose of their tied public houses.

Sometimes companies will reach agreements between themselves covering prices and areas in which each will trade. Such agreements are called *Restrictive Trade Practices* which can be referred to the Restrictive Practices Court by the Director General – with the result that the court will declare them illegal unless the parties to the agreement can convince it otherwise.

CHAPTER 11

The Utilities

*The supply and control of gas, electricity, water and sewerage –
telecommunications and railways*

Public to private

All of the utilities about which this chapter is written were once part of the
public sector. The successive Conservative Thatcher and Major governments
changed all that, through their privatisation programmes. As each utility was
privatised, money was raised from the flotation for the Treasury. In addition,
large numbers of the population became shareholders for the first time. They
also often made a quick profit from state utilities sold at much less than their
true market value (called 'Syds' from the publicity for the British Gas privatisation) – possibly making them more in tune with Conservative
philosophy.

After a certain interval, the Conservative government removed its control
over the future ownership of the utilities, with the result that many are now
wholly or partly in foreign hands – usually French, American or Canadian.

Each privatised utility was given its own *regulator*, charged with protecting
the public interest, since in most cases the utility would remain a monopoly
supplier, now privately-owned and more concerned with the interests of its
shareholders than its customers.

The regulators also have to authorise any price rises, using a formula
linked to the rate of inflation. With the exception of water, all price rises have
to be below the rate of inflation. In the case of water, price rises above the
rate of inflation are permitted because of the greater financial demands on
the water companies to improve their infrastructure to meet the requirements

of the 1990 EU Waste Water Treatment Directive – pumping raw sewage into the sea is no longer an option.

For its part, the Conservative government would have had an interest in ensuring that the privatisation programme was seen to succeed and may not have expected too great an imposition on the new privatised utilities by the regulators.

The New Labour Government realised that the privatisation process could not be reversed, so instead it limited the ability of the privatised utilities to make excess profits from charges, by imposing a one-off 'windfall tax'. It may well also be that with a new government known to be less favourably disposed towards the privatised utilities, the regulators will be encouraged to become more stringent in the way in which they supervise the activities of the utilities.

Gas

The *British Gas Board* was privatised in 1986. For a time, *British Gas plc* continued to be in a monopoly position, having both the means of distribution and the product being supplied. That has now changed as a result of the Gas Act 1995.

British Gas plc had to restructure itself in 1997 (into *BG plc* and *Centrica plc*) to meet the challenge of competition – a single company could not own the pipeline and be a gas supplier at the same time. It also sought to minimise the commercial impact on the more profitable parts of its business from some much earlier fixed-price 'take-and-pay' gas contracts. Over the years since those contracts were first negotiated, the market price of gas from the producers had dropped and British Gas had to buy gas from producers at much greater prices than the current open-market price being paid by its new gas supplier competitors.

Competition had been introduced earlier into the commercial/industrial gas supply market over 2,500 therms. The 1995 Act extended competition in gas supply to residential customers on a phased basis: 1996 – south-west England; 1997 – south-east England; 1998 the rest of England and Scotland. There were difficulties experienced by some customers when they switched away from BG to an alternative supplier – with BG continuing to bill them for gas!

The 1995 Act also introduced a new licensing regime:

- *Public Gas Transporters* (PGT) – companies (such as the BG plc subsidiary, TransCo) operating a pipeline system; and

- *Gas Shippers* – companies who contract with a PGT for their gas to travel through the PGT's pipeline to reach the Gas Suppliers; and

- *Gas Suppliers* – companies (such as BG) who sell gas to consumers.

The whole industry is overseen by the regulator, the *Office of Gas Supply* (OFGAS).

Electricity

When the electricity industry was publicly owned, the generation and national grid side was managed by the *Central Electricity Generating Board* (CEGB) which had responsibility for ensuring that there was sufficient electricity to meet peak demand, especially in winter. Distribution was handled by a series of *regional electricity boards* passing electricity from the national grid to consumers through their own local networks.

Electricity was privatised in 1989 – or some of it was – forming *National Power plc* and *Powergen plc* as conventional generators and a series of privatised *regional electricity companies* (RECs – based on the regional electricity boards) as distributors which also initially owned part of the privatised *National Grid*.

The nuclear power generation part of the industry initially remained in State ownership since it was thought to be unsaleable, because of uncertainty about future decommissioning costs. To make them more palatable for eventual privatisation, in 1996 *Nuclear Electric* and *Scottish Nuclear*, which run the more modern Advanced Gas-cooled (AGC) and Pressurised Water (PWR) nuclear stations, became subsidiaries of *British Energy*. The older Magnox nuclear stations were transferred to *Magnox Electric*, destined to remain in the public sector.

The system in England and Wales is now:

- *Generation* – National Power plc, Powergen plc, British Energy and Magnox Electric;

- *Transmission* – National Grid (NGC); and

- *Distribution* – Regional Electricity Companies (REC)

The position in Scotland is that *ScottishPower plc* and *Scottish Hydro-Electric* generate, transmit and distribute electricity. The two companies are obliged to buy all the output from Scottish Nuclear Ltd. – There is a similar arrangement in Northern Ireland, with *Northern Ireland Electricity plc*, privatised in 1993, undertaking all three rôles.

Electricity is imported by England from Scotland through the National Grid and from France through a cross-Channel cable managed by NGC and *Electricité de France*.

The process of supply involves the generators selling their electricity to suppliers through a market known as 'the Pool'. The National Grid then distributes electricity in bulk across the national grid. In recent winters, there have been fears that the new contract-based system, involving a range of generators, has put the system in danger of voltage reduction ('brown-out') when demand has exceeded expectations.

The distinction between generator and distributor is about to become blurred. In 1998, RECs will lose their monopoly to distribute electricity to franchise customers (using less than 100kW) – from that date, such customers will be able to buy their electricity from their own REC, another REC, a new independent supplier, or even a Generator!

The industry is overseen by the *Director General of Electricity Supply* in the *Office of Electricity Regulation* (OFFER).

Water

Before privatisation, water supply and quality was the responsibility of a range of statutory boards and companies. The government departments involved in overseeing the now privatised water industry are the Department of the Environment/Welsh Office and the Ministry of Agriculture, Fisheries and Food.

The DoE/Welsh Office carries out its part of the statutory structure through three bodies: OFWAT, the Environment Agency and the Drinking Water Inspectorate.

The *Director General of Water Services* (in the Office of Water Services, OFWAT) regulates the economic aspects of the water industry – the level of infrastructure development and the charges to customers (which can be set above the rate of inflation).

The *Environment Agency* (which took over the functions of the *National Rivers Authority* (NRA) in April 1996) regulates the water environment – the management of water resources and pollution control; recreation and conservation. The consent of the Environment Agency is needed for the abstraction of water and the discharge of effluent.

The *Drinking Water Inspectorate* regulates drinking water quality.

The *Ministry of Agriculture, Fisheries and Food*/Welsh Office is responsible for policy relating to land drainage, flood protection, sea defence and the protection and defence of inland and coastal fisheries.

There are 10 water service companies which have statutory responsibilities for the quality and sufficiency of water supply and for sewerage and sewage treatment. There are 19 (originally 29 prior to mergers) supply-only companies, supplying water to nearly 25% of the population.

Water supplied to domestic premises is charged for either on a basis similar to the old rating system (the value of the property) or by metering. Supplies to commercial or industrial premises are metered.

In Scotland, three water authorities (*North, West* and *East of Scotland Water Authorities*) are now responsible for public water supply, sewerage and sewage disposal. The interests of consumers are protected by the *Scottish Water and Sewerage Customers Council*. In April 1996, the *Scottish Environment Protection Agency* took over responsibility for water pollution control from the Scottish river purification authorities.

The *Department of the Environment for Northern Ireland* is responsible for public water supply, sewerage, conservation and river cleanliness throughout that country.

Telecommunications

Before privatisation, telecommunications were originally the responsibility of the Post Office (Post Office Telephones) and later a State-owned monopoly *British Telecommunications plc* (British Telecom – BT). BT was privatised in 1984.

Until 1991, only two companies, BT and *Mercury Communications Ltd* (part of the Cable & Wireless Group and 20% owned by Bell Canada Enterprises) were permitted to operate telecommunication systems – a so-called 'duopoly'. Mercury constructed its own long-distance all-digital network, which now links 90 cities and towns across the UK and can provide a service to the whole population, using BT's local line network.

There are now about 150 licensed telecommunications operators in the UK – including 125 cable operators, 19 regional and national public telecommunications operators and four mobile operators.

In spite of this increased competition, BT is still by far the largest operator, with 27 million residential and business lines, handling over 103 million local, national and international calls a day.

The industry is regulated by the *Office of Telecommunications* (OFTEL) under the *Director General of Telecommunications*, who checks that licence conditions are followed, ensures that operators (especially BT with its pre-eminent position) behave fairly in the competitive regime, deals with complaints and provides advice to the President of the Board of Trade (DTI).

Railways

The railways system in the UK, which began in 1825 with the Stockton & Darlington Railway, was developed by a series of independent companies. In 1948, the system was nationalised, to be co-ordinated and controlled by the State-owned *British Railways Board* (BR).

Although some rationalisation of the system took place in the 1960s ('Dr Beeching's Axe' fell on many small branch-lines), it still remained a single integrated system – until recently.

Under the Railways Act 1993, the Conservative government set about privatising the system against a background of widespread concern about the results which might ensue from the fragmentation of the system.

The process of privatisation was much more complex than earlier privatisations and involved:

- splitting track and signalling infrastructure from train operations;

- making a new company, Railtrack, responsible for infrastructure;

- retaining train operations with BR until they could be sold off or franchised;

- privatising Railtrack;

- selling off BR's freight and parcels operations to the private sector;

- franchising BR's passenger services, on a piecemeal basis, to the private sector;

- leasing some stations to private companies;

- appointing a *Rail Regulator* to supervise access to Railtrack's infrastructure; and

- appointing a *Franchising Director* (in OPRAF), to negotiate, award and monitor the franchises; and to pay public subsidies.

BR restructured its passenger services into 25 train operating units, to facilitate privatisation through franchises. Railtrack was privatised in May 1996. BR's freight and parcels operations _ *Transrail, Mainline* and *Loadhaul* (trainload freight); *Red Star* (parcels); *Rail Express Systems* (Royal Mail trains); and *Freightliner* (containers) _ have all been sold to private sector companies.

Since privatisation, some of the issues which have emerged are:

- some inflexible and, at times, bizarre pricing and ticketing arrangements, especially affecting through-ticketing;

- when an accident happens, a process akin to 'pass the parcel' appears to operate between the various companies now involved;

- rail franchises were sold to bus companies, raising questions about true commitment to developing rail services;

- some franchise companies have reduced their costs by cutting staff, which results in large-scale cancellations and poor performance;

- the franchise companies receive such large State subsidies that the fines imposed by OPRAF do not really hurt the companies involved; and

- integrating public transport in urban areas to reduce car-usage is harder to achieve.

CHAPTER 12

The Treasury

The Treasury – the regulation of investment services – the Bank of England – the annual budget process – basic financial terms

The Treasury

Her Majesty's Treasury is one of the Great Offices of State – its importance is emphasised by the fact that the Prime Minister is First Lord of the Treasury. The Treasury has the primary responsibility for formulating and implementing national economic policy. However, there are others involved – the Bank of England and some other government departments, notably the Department of Trade and Industry; and other bodies such as the Office of Fair Trading and the Monopolies and Mergers Commission.

The economy is complex and the government keeps in touch with developments through informal links with the industrial, commercial and financial sectors. Apart from any other sources of advice, the Chancellor of the Exchequer receives a twice-yearly report from the Panel of Independent Forecasters on the current state of the economy and its future prospects.

Final responsibility for the broad thrust of economic policy rests, like other aspects of major government policy, with the Cabinet.

The Treasury is also responsible for legislation which regulates banks, building societies, friendly societies and investment business.

The regulation of investment business

The Treasury supervises the *Securities and Investments Board* (SIB) which has statutory responsibilities under the Financial Services Act 1986 for the regulation of investment business.

With the demutualisation of some building societies and insurance companies and the complexity of some modern financial products, the financial regulation regime is falling behind the sector it was designed to regulate. In addition, there has been a series of scandals (the mis-selling of pensions is one) which have called into question the efficacy of the present regulation arrangements, which involve a large degree of self-regulation. The New Labour Government has announced its intention of simplifying the regulation scene – by increasing SIB's own powers at the expense of the other regulatory bodies – creating a 'Super-SIB'.

For the present, SIB is responsible for recognising 'front-line' regulators: either self-regulating organisations (SROs) or recognised professional bodies (RPBs). The SROs are:

- the *Investment Management Regulatory Organisation* (IMRO) – supervises fund management firms;

- the *Securities and Futures Authority* (SFA) – supervises the London Stock Exchange, futures brokers and dealers and Eurobond dealers; and

- the *Personal Investment Authority* (PIA) – supervises firms providing independent financial advice to individuals and marketing financial products to their clients.

The Bank of England

The Bank of England ('The Old Lady of Threadneedle Street') was founded in 1694 by Royal Charter and Act of Parliament. Its capital stock was acquired by the government in 1946 and it is, in effect, the UK *Central Bank*.

The rôle of the Bank of England is to maintain a stable and efficient monetary and financial framework within which the UK economy can operate. In doing so, the Bank acts as the Treasury's agent in managing the UK gold and foreign exchange reserves and manages the government's debt by selling 'gilt-edged' government stock.

The Bank also has the sole right in England and Wales to issue banknotes, backed by the government. In Scotland there are three banks which issue banknotes and four such banks in Northern Ireland.

It used to be the case that the Chancellor of the Exchequer took decisions about interest rates, as a political issue, which the Bank then implemented. Shortly after the New Labour Government came into power, the Chancellor of the Exchequer announced that, in future, responsibility for deciding interest rates would be a technical rather than a political one and would, instead, rest with the Governor of the Bank of England and a special *Monetary Policy Committee.*

However, things did not go all in the Bank's favour – as a result of some previous spectacular bank scandals, notably Barings Bank, the Chancellor announced shortly afterwards that the Bank would lose some of its existing responsibilities to supervise the UK retail and wholesale banking system under the Banking Act 1967 – these would become the responsibility of the new 'Super-SIB' mentioned in the previous section.

The annual budget process

The UK budget system changed in November 1993 when a unified Budget arrangement was introduced – under which the government presents to Parliament its taxation proposals for the next financial year beginning 5 April and its spending proposals for the next three years.

These proposals are presented to the Commons by the Chancellor of the Exchequer in November each year, in the Budget Statement, which is followed by a series of resolutions which form the basis of a Finance Bill produced the following January. Some of the tax changes can take effect immediately the Chancellor announces them, in advance of the Finance Bill, as authorised by the Provisional Collection of Taxes Act 1968.

During February to April prior to the Budget, each government department will have prepared its own estimates and submitted them to the Treasury for approval. An overall target for government spending will have been set earlier and the final determination of departmental allocations within the overall target takes place in the *Public Expenditure Survey*, which is announced at the same time as the Budget.

There can be so-called 'mini-budgets', at any time of the year, when the Chancellor of the Exchequer thinks appropriate. There was a mini-budget at the beginning of July 1997, when the New Labour Government presented its first budget after coming into office.

The annual budget process is likely to change again, because New Labour Chancellor Gordon Brown announced his intention to bring the UK financial year (6 April to 5 April) into line with the calendar year in time for the millennium. The process will start by the 1998 budget being presented in the last week of February or the first week of March 1998, preceded by an Autumn Statement in November 1997. The transition will be achieved by the 1998/99 financial year ending on 5 April 1999 as usual, but the following transitional financial year, 1999/2000, will last only nine months – until 31 December 1999.

Some basic terms defined

The UK economy is *market-based*, involving the buying and selling of goods and services within the UK and the rest of the World. The concept of a market is based upon supply and demand – ideally, the most stable market is where the supply of goods matches the demand for them. The present approach to economic policy in the UK is to expose as much of the economy as possible to market-forces, avoiding the use of direct controls on pay, prices, foreign exchange and commercial credit.

The ideal balance is never achieved. If supply exceeds demand, then prices will generally fall – good news for the consumer in the short-term, but bad news for the supplier/manufacturer who might go out of business. If demand exceeds supply, then there will be too much money chasing too few goods and prices will tend to rise – good news for the supplier (who will try to raise production) but bad news for the consumer, because increased prices also means inflation in the economy.

Inflation in the economy is expressed in terms of the percentage rise in the *Retail Prices Index* (RPI), which records the price of goods and services purchased by households. A variant of the RPI is one which excludes mortgage payments – called *'underlying inflation'*. The rate of inflation is one of the key indicators to the health of the economy – so key, in fact, that the Bank of England produces a *Quarterly Inflation Report* which is used as a basis for monetary control and interest rates.

All developed economies involve trade with other countries – exporting and importing goods and services. The EU is now the UK's most important trading partner. There will always be some difference between the value of goods and services exported and those imported – the *Balance of Payments*.

Goods are not the only commodity exported – exports also include services, the so-called *'invisible exports'*, such as financial and insurance services and investment income transactions. Invisible exports are always in surplus and are an important component in calculating the net position on the *Balance of Trade* with the rest of the World.

If the value of exports exceeds imports, then the Balance of Payments are said to be *in surplus*; if imports exceed exports, then there is said to be a Balance of Payments *deficit*. The Balance of Payments is usually expressed as a *current account* position. The current account basis includes trade in goods and services, including finance, tourism, transport and transactions in investment income and transfers. Less often, a *capital account* position is quoted – this includes inward and outward investment in the UK, external borrowing and lending by UK residents and changes in the UK official reserves. At present, the UK Balance of Payments is in deficit and although the figures look enormous (1995 – £2,900 million), they represent less than 1% of the GDP.

Gross Domestic Product (GDP) is the value of all goods and services produced in the UK economy, after offsetting the cost of imported goods and services. *Gross National Product* (GNP) is the GDP plus net property income from overseas investments.

GDP and GNP can be expressed in more than one way: either in terms of market prices (the prices actually paid by people for goods and services) or at factor cost (the cost of goods and services before adding taxes and deducting subsidies). *National Income* is the GNP at factor cost, minus capital consumption. The figures can also be expressed at different price bases: current prices or constant prices (removing the effect of inflation).

So, the 1995 UK GDP at market prices was £700,890 million and at factor cost was £604,259 million. The 1995 UK GNP was £710,462 million at market prices and £613,831 million at factor cost. The 1995 UK National Income was £540,643 million.

General Government Expenditure (GGE) is the total of central and local government expenditure, including support for nationalised industries and other public corporations. At present the level of GGE is at just over 40% of National Income.

Government expenditure is financed through taxation and borrowing. If the economy is performing well (that is, not in recession), then more of government expenditure can be financed through taxation, reducing the need to borrow to make up the shortfall. The amount which the government needs to borrow is expressed as the *Public Sector Borrowing Requirement* (PSBR). In 1995 the PSBR was about 5% of GDP – the aim of the Conservative government was to reduce this to 0% by the end of the 1990s – that is, in balance.

The taxation levied by government can be of two kinds – direct and indirect. Direct taxation is levied 'directly' on an individual's or body's *income* – such as Income Tax or Corporation Tax. *Indirect Taxation* is paid 'indirectly' on *expenditure* by an individual when, for example, purchasing goods – such as Value Added Tax (VAT) or Customs and Excise duties.

Taxes are regarded as more fair, *'progressive'*, if they are linked in some way to the individual's ability to pay them – such as Income Tax. Taxes which are not so linked to ability to pay are likely to have harsh consequences for the less well-off and are criticised as being *'regressive'* – the most notable recent example of a deeply unpopular regressive tax was the Community Charge (the Poll Tax) introduced by Mrs Thatcher – it was so unpopular that it had to abandoned after a short period.

CHAPTER 13

The Home Office

The rôle of the Home Office – the criminal justice system – the treatment of offenders – immigration and asylum

The Home Office

The *Department for Home Affairs* (the Home Office) is supervised by the *Secretary of State for Home Affairs* (the Home Secretary). Like the Treasury and the Foreign and Commonwealth Office, it is one of the Great Offices of State. Apart from other responsibilities, the Home Secretary advises the Sovereign on the exercise of the Royal Prerogative of Mercy.

Although the main responsibilities of the Home Office are to do with the criminal justice system, it has other responsibilities such as elections, race relations, immigration and asylum.

As far as *elections* are concerned, the rôle of the Home Office is almost entirely one of overall supervision, since the various aspects of the electoral system are dealt with by others – electoral registration and the conduct of elections are the responsibility of local authorities and electoral boundary review is the responsibility of the Boundary Commissions.

As far as *race relations* are concerned, previous legislation was strengthened by the Race Relations Act 1976, which outlawed various forms of racial discrimination and gave access to various forms of redress. The Public Order Act 1986 made the incitement of racial hatred a criminal offence.

A quango, the *Commission for Racial Equality* (CRE), investigates alleged unlawful racial discrimination and can issue non-discrimination notices to stop discriminatory practices. The CRE also issues Codes of Practice aimed at promoting good practice.

The criminal justice system

The criminal justice system has two aspects – the courts and the treatment of offenders sentenced by the courts. The Home Office is concerned with the treatment of offenders.

The court system is overseen by the Lord Chancellor, who is head of the judiciary and a senior member of the Cabinet – with the day-to-day work being undertaken for the Lord Chancellor's Department by the Court Service, an executive agency. The Lord Chancellor has responsibility for promoting any general reforms of the *civil* law and for the legal aid system.

The Attorney-General and the Solicitor-General are the government's main legal advisers and they can represent the Crown in the more important domestic and international cases. They are members of the Commons and their posts carry ministerial status.

The Attorney-General also has ultimate responsibility for *enforcing* the criminal law, with the Solicitor-General effectively acting as his deputy. The Attorney-General also supervises the Director of Public Prosecutions (DPP) who runs the Crown Prosecution Service (CPS), the Director of the Serious Fraud Office (SFO) and the DPP for Northern Ireland.

The Home Secretary has overall responsibility for *criminal* law and will introduce any Bills required to change it. The police service, the probation service and the prison system are all services under the overall supervision of the Home Office. The Home Secretary is, in effect, the Police Authority for London, supervising the Metropolitan Police Commissioner. Outside the metropolis, the police service is managed by a series of Chief Constables, reporting to their local Police Authority (as described in *Essential Local Government*). The Probation Service is managed by a series of Chief Probation Officers, reporting to their local Probation Committee.

The prisons in England and Wales are managed somewhat more directly by the Home Office, but through the *Prison Service*, an executive agency of the Home Office, with its own Chief Executive. Similar executive agencies exist in Scotland and Northern Ireland. The use of an executive agency means that it is the Prison Service Chief Executive who is responsible for administrative mistakes, rather than the Home Secretary *(see section on Ministerial responsibility in Chapter 3)*.

In Scotland, the Secretary of State is responsible for criminal law, crime prevention, police, prisons and legal aid.

Treatment of offenders

Offenders, if convicted, receive either a non-custodial or a custodial sentence.

Non-custodial sentences include: fines, compensation orders, probation orders, supervision orders, community service orders, and combination orders (elements of probation and community service). In England and Wales, the *Probation Service* will be involved in monitoring non-custodial offenders during the life of a probation, supervision or community service order. In Scotland, similar work is undertaken by local authority social work departments.

Custodial sentences will be served in prison – with varying degrees of security ranging from an open prison to a high security prison – or in a young offender institution.

Consistent with the Conservative government's policy of privatising as much of the public services as possible, the Criminal Justice Act 1991 authorised the Home Secretary to contract out to the private sector the management of prisons and the escort of prisoners outside prison. The escort services were privatised with initial criticism of the quality of their service – including the loss of some prisoners. Four new prisons, as they were completed (The Wolds, Humberside; Blakenhurst, Worcestershire; Doncaster; and Buckley Hall, Rochdale) were put out to private sector management, but are still part of the Prison Service.

In addition, the *Private Finance Initiative* (PFI) has been used for financing, designing, building and managing three new prisons in England and Wales (Merseyside, Nottinghamshire and South Wales) and one in Scotland (Kilmarnock) – to be opened 1989-99.

Early release of prisoners – England and Wales

The Criminal Justice Act 1991 reformed the sentence remission and parole arrangements in England and Wales, with the Parole Board advising the Home Secretary on the early release of long-term prisoners.

The arrangements involved the early release of prisoners sentenced to less than four years, after they had served half of their sentence. Prisoners serving four years or more could be released early after serving half of their sentence if approved by the Parole Board and automatically after serving two-thirds of their sentence. The Parole Board had the final decision on prisoners serving more than four but less than seven years; and made recommendations to the Home Secretary on those serving longer sentences.

All prisoners on parole who were originally sentenced to one year or more, were let out of prison on licence (under supervision by the Probation Service) until the three-quarters point of their sentence.

Prisoners sentenced to life imprisonment for certain kinds of murder – murder of police and prison officers; terrorist murder; murder in the course of robbery using firearms; and sadistic murder of children – usually have to serve at least 20 years. The release of mandatory life prisoners on licence is authorised only by the Home Secretary on the recommendation of the Parole Board and after the judiciary have been consulted.

Prisoners sentenced to life imprisonment for offences other than murder would be released by the Home Secretary (if directed by the Parole Board to do so) after a period set by the judge at the trial. The Parole Board has to decide whether or not continued confinement in prison is needed to protect the public.

If a prisoner who has been released early commits another offence while on parole, the trial judge at the subsequent trial may order the offender to serve all or part of the outstanding original sentence as well.

The purpose of parole is to give prisoners something to look forward to and to encourage good behaviour in prison by paroling those with a good record of conduct.

However, in April 1996, the Conservative government under Home Secretary Michael Howard decided to issue a White Paper *'Protecting the Public'* as part of its 'get tough with crime' policy – possibly with the forthcoming General Election in mind. The proposals in that White Paper were:

- an automatic life sentence would be imposed on an offender convicted for a second time of a serious sexual or violent offence;

- mandatory minimum prison sentences would be imposed on drug dealers and burglars for repeat offences; and

- automatic early release and parole would be abolished, with prisoners serving the full term of their sentence, unless they earned up to 20% off their sentence for good behaviour; those sentenced to one year or more and released early would be supervised by the Probation Service for a period equal to 15% of their original sentence.

These proposals attracted much criticism – especially from all parts of the criminal justice system, including the judiciary – not least because the same Conservative government in an earlier 1990 White Paper had said *"...nobody now regards imprisonment as an effective means of reform...".*

The prison population was already high, with adverse conditions in over-crowded prisons leading to more internal disturbances and with the need to build ever-more new prisons. The Home Office even imported a prison ship from the USA at great expense because it could not build new prisons fast enough. The new policy would increase the number of prisoners retained in the prison system, leading to yet more demand for additional prison places.

However, most of these changes were included in the Crime (Sentences) Act 1997. All prisoners have to serve the full sentence. However, those serving less than three years could gain, and lose, 'early release days'. Those serving three years or more could be released on Parole Board recommendation after serving five-sixths of the sentence. New Labour may change this.

Early release of prisoners – Scotland and Northern Ireland

The arrangements in Scotland are broadly similar, but there are differences. The Parole Board can release prisoners serving between four and 10 years, after they have served half of their sentence. The early release of those serving more than 10 years needs the consent of the Secretary of State. Those released early from sentences of four years or more are supervised to the end of their sentence. Parolees are supervised by local authority social work departments.

In Northern Ireland, special arrangements are in place for terrorist offences. Terrorists sentenced to five years or more can usually be paroled only after serving two-thirds of their sentence – but this was changed in November 1995 to bring it in line with the rest of the UK; parole after serving half of the sentence. If a terrorist is convicted of another terrorist offence before the expiry of the original sentence, then the original sentence has to be completed before the next one starts.

Oversight of the prison system

Each prison and young offender institution has a *Board of Visitors* – volunteers from the local community appointed by the Home Secretary. A similar arrangement, involving a visiting committee reporting to the Secretary of State operates in Scotland. The Board of Visitors visits prisons and hears complaints from prisoners.

There are independent *Prisons Inspectorates*, reporting to the Home Secretary and the Scottish Secretary of State, which visit each prison about every three years to report on prison conditions and the treatment of prisoners.

The Prison Service has its own internal request and complaints system and prisoners still dissatisfied after using it can complain to the independent *Prisons Ombudsman.*

Immigration and asylum

The immigration of people into the UK is regulated by the Immigration Act 1971 and the statutory Rules made under it.

British citizens and those Commonwealth citizens who had the right of abode before January 1983, retain the right of abode in the UK and are not subject to immigration control.

Nationals of the European Economic Area (EEA), which is the EU plus Iceland, Liechtenstein and Norway, are not subject to significant immigration control. They may work in the UK and, if able to support themselves, also have the right to reside in the UK.

Nationals of specified countries require a visa before they may enter the UK. All other nationals subject to immigration control need entry clearance before coming to the UK to work or live.

People fleeing from persecution or refugees can seek asylum in the UK – in accordance with the United Nations Protocol on the Status of Refugees. The Conservative government decided that too many people were trying to enter the UK as 'refugees' – many were called 'economic refugees' after a better lifestyle, to suggest that they were not real refugees. So, the Asylum and Immigration Act 1996 was passed – enabling the government to designate countries as not giving rise to a serious risk of persecution and, therefore, people coming from those countries could not be refugees; some of the government's designations brought criticism about what factors had been taken into account.

In addition, the same Act also modified the appeal arrangements so that appeals can only be made after repatriation from the UK – some would say that such a limited right of appeal was all but useless.

CHAPTER 14

Culture, Media and Sport

The rôle of the Department of Culture, Media and Sport – the arts – media – National Lottery – heritage – sport

The Department of Culture, Media and Sport

The Secretary of State for Culture, Media and Sport is a member of the Cabinet. The Department's responsibilities include support for the arts, heritage and sport and the regulation of the film industry, broadcasting, the press, the National Lottery and the export licensing of antiques. The Department was previously called the Department of National Heritage.

The Secretaries of State for Scotland, Wales and Northern Ireland have responsibilities for arts in their respective countries.

Arts

The Department determines government policy on support for the arts and supervises expenditure on national museums and art galleries, by the *Arts Council of England*, and by the *National Library*.

Planned central government expenditure on the arts through the Department in 1996/97 was £937 million, of which £186 million was spent via the Arts Council. This money is mostly spent on supporting the performing and visual arts. Grants are made to the *British Film Institute*, the *Crafts Council* and to the *National Heritage Memorial Fund* – the aim of the Fund is to help bodies who want to buy (for the public benefit) land, buildings, works of art and other objects connected with the national heritage. Quite often a grant from the Fund helps to keep a particularly important work of art in the UK when it would otherwise have been exported.

The *Arts Council* is a quango and aims: to develop and improve the knowledge, understanding and practice of the arts; to make the arts more accessible; and to advise and co-operate with central and local government and other organisations. Direct financial support and advice is given to major arts centres and opera, drama and dance companies (such as Royal Opera, Royal Ballet, English National Opera and the Royal Shakespeare Company) – and to touring companies as well. Individual creative artists and writers are also supported.

The 10 *Regional Arts Boards* also offer similar support to the arts, but on a regional basis – complementing the support from the Arts Council itself.

Broadcast media

In relation to the broadcast media, the rôle of the Department is essentially one of overall policy and supervision of the broadcasting *system*. However, the Broadcasting Act 1990 enables the government to intervene when programme content issues such as taste and decency are involved. Unacceptable foreign satellite services receivable in the UK can be (and have been) banned by the government – anyone supporting such services in the UK can be prosecuted for a criminal offence.

In the case of television and radio, three public bodies work to broad requirements and objectives approved by Parliament:

- *British Broadcasting Corporation* (BBC) – the UK's main public service broadcaster in television and radio, under its latest Royal Charter granted in 1996, funded by the annual licence fee collected by TV Licensing, a subsidiary of the Post Office;

- *Independent Television Commission* (ITC) – licensing and regulating commercial television services, including cable and satellite; and

- *Radio Authority* – licensing and regulating commercial radio services, including cable and satellite.

Through the Broadcasting Act 1996, the government introduced a new regulatory framework for digital (as opposed to analogue) terrestrial broadcasting for both commercial and public service broadcasting.

Press media

The regulation of the press media is still voluntary – through the *Press Complaints Commission* set up by the newspaper and periodical industry. The

Commission consists of newspaper and magazine representatives and people from outside the industry.

The Commission deals with complaints by members of the public about the content and conduct of newspapers and magazines; and operates a code of practice agreed with editors concerning respect for privacy, opportunity to reply, corrections, journalist behaviour, references to race and religion, payments to criminals for articles, and protection of confidential sources.

The government published a White Paper *'Privacy and Media Intrusion: the Government's Response'* in 1995 – explicitly rejecting calls for the statutory regulation of the press.

Media Ownership

The Broadcasting Act 1990 provided a detailed framework under which the regulatory bodies (the ITC and the Radio Authority) could keep ownership of the broadcasting media dispersed – and prevent undue concentrations of single and cross-media ownership, especially by companies based outside the EU.

The Broadcasting Act 1996 relaxed the media ownership rules within, and across, different media sectors. There is now a set of 'public interest' criteria which enable the regulatory bodies to allow or reject mergers or acquisitions between newspapers and television and radio companies.

The previous two-licence limit on ITV licences has been replaced by a 'television ownership limit' of a 15% share of the total television audience. In addition, local newspapers with more than a 50% share of their market can now own a local radio station, but only if there is at least one other independent radio station operating in that area.

The National Lottery

The National Lottery was launched in November 1994 and is run by a private company, *Camelot Group plc*, who won the contract. The Lottery is regulated by the *Director-General of the National Lottery* in the *Office of the National Lottery* (OFLOT).

There has been criticism of the way in which the Lottery is run and the level of the profits made by Camelot plc. Camelot plc has said that it will co-operate with suggestions from the New Labour Government that the Lottery should be run on a non-profit-making basis in the future.

Voluntary organisations and charities have also complained that the level of donations which they would normally expect to receive has dropped significantly, because people are spending their money on lottery tickets instead, in the belief that the money will find its way to the charities through the Lottery's 'good causes'. Evidence has been produced that grants from the National Lotteries Charities Board have not made up the shortfall.

There have also been criticisms that in most regions of the country there is little correlation between the amount spent on the lottery and the amount returned on 'good causes' within the region. The South East has benefited particularly generously, with large grants being made to prestigious arts venues for which most ordinary people could not afford to buy tickets. The New Labour Minister has indicated that he will expect those venues to produce proposals for making themselves more accessible to the general public.

The money which goes into the Lottery emerges as follows:

Prizes	50%
'Good causes'	28%
Tax	12%
Retailer Commission	5%
Operating Costs and Camelot plc profit	5%

The 28% 'good causes' proceeds are divided equally between the five 'good causes': the arts, sport, heritage, charities and projects to mark the millennium. In the first year of the Lottery's operation, £1,200 million was awarded to 'good causes'. Since April 1996 Lottery funds can be spent not only on buildings and equipment but also on projects which develop people's talents and potential.

The 'good causes' Lottery money is distributed by the following bodies:

- *arts* – the Arts Councils of England, Wales and Northern Ireland and the Scottish Arts Council;

- *sports* – the English Sports Council, the Sports Councils of Wales and Northern Ireland and the Scottish Sports Council;

- *heritage* – the National Heritage Memorial Fund;

- *charities* – the National Lottery Charities Board; and

- *projects to mark the millennium* – the Millennium Commission.

Heritage

The Department has responsibility for the maintenance of the royal palaces and parks open to the public – which is carried out by two executive agencies: *Historic Royal Palaces* and the *Royal Parks Agency*.

The Department also has responsibility for the care of over 400 properties of special architectural or historic interest or which are ancient monuments. Again, the responsibilities are carried out by an executive agency – *English Heritage*. English Heritage also provides advice to the Department on how to deal with applications to demolish or alter scheduled monuments or listed buildings.

In Scotland, the executive agency *Historic Scotland* provides a similar service to the Secretary of State. In Wales, the executive agency *Cadw* provides support for the Secretary of State there.

The *National Heritage Memorial Fund*, as a grant-aiding body and as a distributor of the heritage share of the Lottery proceeds, has already been mentioned.

Sport

The Secretary of State is responsible for government policy on sport and recreation in England. The Secretaries of State for Scotland, Wales and Northern Ireland have similar responsibilities.

National sports policy is led by the Secretary of State, in association with the three other Secretaries of State.

Sports policy and advice is delivered through the five quangos appointed by the relevant Secretaries of State – the Sports Councils: the *English Sports Council* (ESC), the *Sports Council for Wales*, the *Scottish Sports Council,* the *Sports Council for Northern Ireland* and the *United Kingdom Sports Council* (UKSC). The rôle of UKSC is strategic planning and co-ordination – including representing UK interests overseas and trying to bring major sporting events to the UK.

The *National Sports Medicine Institute*, based at the medical college at St Bart's Hospital in London is jointly funded by UKSC and ESC.

Finally, spectator safety is the responsibility of the Department, which jointly with the Scottish Office, published its *'Guide to Safety at Sports Grounds'* which is used by local authorities when issuing safety certificates to licensed sports grounds.

CHAPTER 15

International Relations and Defence

The rôle of the Foreign and Commonwealth Office – the Secretary of State for International Development – UN – NATO – UK defence strategy – the Ministry of Defence

The Foreign and Commonwealth Office

The Foreign and Commonwealth Office (FCO) is the government department in charge of the UK's overall foreign policy and is headed by the Foreign and Commonwealth Secretary (the Foreign Secretary), who is a senior member of the Cabinet.

Before the New Labour Government, the Foreign Secretary was assisted by five Ministers, none of whom had Cabinet rank, and one of whom was the *Minister for Overseas Development*, responsible for the *Overseas Development Administration* (ODA), part of the FCO. As will be seen from Appendix A, that has changed – there is now a *Secretary of State for International Development*, effectively turning the ODA into a new *Department for International Development* (DfID) and the number of FCO Ministers has dropped to four.

These changes are clearly intended to be more than cosmetic and may lead to significant shifts in what the new department does, but, until the effect of those changes becomes clear, this chapter assumes that the new DfID will continue the existing work of the ODA – that may need to be updated.

The *Diplomatic Service* within the FCO is headed by a career civil servant, the Permanent Under Secretary of State at the FCO, who also provides foreign policy advice to the Foreign Secretary.

The FCO maintains diplomatic or consular relations with 188 countries and has diplomatic missions at nine international organisations or conferences (such as the UN). The main rôle of UK embassies abroad is to act as a local point of contact in the formal diplomatic relations between the UK and that country. However, the embassy also provides a range of consular services, aimed at protecting the interests of UK citizens within that country, especially when they encounter difficulties. There is also a significant emphasis on the promotion of the UK as a trading partner and some embassy staff – commercial attachés – will be devoted to this activity.

People seeking entry into the UK and who are subject to immigration control and require pre-entry clearance, obtain that clearance from the visa section or consulate of the local FCO mission in their country.

The FCO has one executive agency – *Wilton Park International Conference Centre*, West Sussex – which organises conferences on international problems, involving politicians, academics, professionals and business people, often from abroad.

Other government departments and bodies

The FCO (and DfID) are not the only government departments interested in international relations.

The *Ministry of Defence* (MoD) obviously maintains the UK armed forces, but it is also responsible for military liaison with the UK's allies – in NATO and elsewhere.

The *Department of Trade and Industry* (DTI) influences international trade policy and commercial relations with other countries. The FCO and DTI jointly run an export promotion body – *Overseas Trade Services* – with staff based overseas in FCO diplomatic missions and in the UK at the DTI in London, in regional offices and in Business Links (a DTI programme aimed at supporting the development of small firms).

In relation to Europe, the FCO co-ordinates UK EU policy through the *Cabinet Office European Secretariat*.

The *British Council* is the UK's principal agency for cultural relations and has 228 offices in 109 overseas countries. The British Council's aims are to promote a wider knowledge of the UK and the English language. The Council does this through encouraging, and in some cases financing, cultural, scientific, technological and educational co-operation between the UK and other countries. One of the more significant activities of the Council is supporting educational exchanges, especially in Europe, through its *Central Bureau for Educational Visits and Exchanges.*

The UK aid programme – the DfID

The principal rôle of the DfID is the delivery of the UK international aid programme, which amounted to £2,314 million in 1994-95, the sixth largest in the world. Most of the countries receiving aid are 'developing countries', but there is now a special category – 'countries in transition' – which covers the emerging democracies in Central and Eastern Europe and the former USSR whose economies are in transition from centrally-managed to market-based.

The UK aid is either given directly by the DfID or is allocated through international bodies such as the EU, UN or the World Bank. Local private sector investment in developing countries is encouraged by the DfID itself and through another government agency, the *Commonwealth Development Corporation* (CDC). The CDC provides loans, equity funds and management services for viable local enterprises in such things as agriculture, industry, transport and housing in over 50 such countries.

Some of the DfID aid is applied through programmes administered by the British Council and a variety of UK charities, such as Oxfam and Save the Children Fund.

The current objectives of the DfID aid programme are:

- *Good government:* By promoting democracy, human rights and the rule of law and by helping governments to become more competent and accountable;

- *Reducing poverty:* By supporting rural development, urban slum clearance and the provision of health, family planning and education services for poor people;

- *Education:* By supporting programmes which enable students and trainees to come to the UK to complete their education and training and by targeting aid to developing countries to improve their own primary and tertiary education systems as envisaged by the 1990 World Conference on 'Education for All';

- *Health:* By improving the effectiveness and coverage of local health services, particularly for women and children, and by promoting special programmes such as those aimed at population and reproductive health following the International Conference on Population and Development in Cairo in 1994;

- *Gender equality:* By supporting the advancement of women in poorer countries through greater access for women and girls to education, health and income, with the long term aim of gender equality, as envisaged by the Fourth World Conference on Women in Peking in 1995;

- *The Environment:* By promoting the protection and sustainable management of the environment, for example through contributing to the Global Environment Facility (GEF), a £2,000 million trust fund to provide help in four areas: climate change, biodiversity, pollution of international waters and protection of the ozone layer. This activity reinforces other similar initiatives – the Convention on Climate Change at the 1992 Earth Summit, limiting the emission of greenhouse gases; the Montreal Protocol Multilateral Fund, phasing out ozone-depleting substances; and the Rio Biodiversity Convention on halting the loss of animal and plant species and the preservation of genetic resources;

- *Natural Resources:* By helping developing countries to promote sustainable and efficient management of their renewable resources in such areas as small-scale agriculture, animal production, fisheries and forestry – the DfID's scientific executive agency, the *Natural Resources Institute*, provides a multi-disciplinary centre of expert advice; and

- *Emergency Relief:* By providing humanitarian aid to meet local emergencies and for disaster relief – co-ordinated through the DfID's *Disaster Unit*.

The Commonwealth

The Commonwealth is of special importance to the UK. It is a voluntary association of 53 member states most of which were previously UK territories. Mozambique, a former Portuguese colony, was permitted to join in November 1995 because it was effectively surrounded by Commonwealth states and wished to join them in membership. South Africa rejoined in 1994, after 33 years of absence. There is mounting pressure from other states who see some benefit from Commonwealth membership, even though they were never UK territories.

The Queen is Head of the Commonwealth and is Head of State of 15 of the member states, besides the UK.

The organisation carries out its work through: a biennial *Meeting of Heads of Government* held at different locations throughout the Commonwealth (the UK hosted the 1997 Meeting – for the first time in 20 years); special conferences of ministers and officials; and diplomatic representatives known as 'High Commissioners'.

The *Commonwealth Secretariat* is based in London and effectively administers the various Commonwealth meetings and conferences, including the *Commonwealth Fund for Technical Co-operation* which arranges consultancy services and training awards for developing countries within the Commonwealth.

The *Commonwealth Games* are not only the most important sporting event taking place within the ambit of the Commonwealth, but also symbolise its qualities as an international organisation for mutual co-operation and development.

United Nations

The UK is a founder member of the United Nations (UN), which in 1945 replaced the League of Nations formed after the First World War. The UK contributes to the UN budget and provides assistance in UN peacekeeping activities. The UN's headquarters are in New York and at present it has 184 countries in membership. New member countries can be admitted on a two-thirds vote by the General Assembly, on a recommendation of the Security Council.

The UN's *Charter* includes a set of principles and purposes, including: the maintenance of international peace and security; the development of friendly relations among nations; the achievement of international co-operation on economic, social, cultural and humanitarian issues; and the protection of human rights and fundamental freedoms.

The main elements of the UN are the General Assembly, the Security Council, the Economic and Social Council, the International Court of Justice and the UN Secretariat.

The *General Assembly* is the main deliberative body, where each member state has one vote. On issues such as peace, security and the budget, decisions require a two-thirds majority – other decisions require a simple majority.

The General Assembly also sets up agencies and programmes to carry its recommendations, especially on humanitarian issues – UN Conference on Trade and Development (UNCTAD), UN International Childrens Emergency Fund (UNICEF) and UN Development Programme (UNDP). UNICEF is probably the most widely-known and was set up in 1946, as a temporary measure only. Since that time UNICEF has proved its worth and is now a permanent organisation with a much wider brief – covering nutrition; drinking water; sanitation; health and welfare; education, training and literacy; and children's rights.

The *Security Council* has the principal task of maintaining peace and security, which it does through a combination of mediation and intervention – peacekeeping effort; peacekeeping operations (usually multinational); and economic sanctions. For example, the multinational force which carried out *Operation Desert Shield* and *Operation Desert Storm* against Iraq operated under a UN mandate.

The Security Council has 15 members, five permanent and 10 elected by the General Assembly for a period of two years. The UK is one of the five permanent members of the *Security Council* – the other four being China, France, Russia and the USA. Important decisions require nine out of the 15 votes – and all five permanent members must support the decision, giving each permanent member an effective veto.

The 54 members of the *Economic and Social Council* (ECOSOC) meet annually to co-ordinate the work of the UN and related agencies such as the World Health Organisation (WHO) and UNESCO, which promotes educational, cultural and social links between nations.

The UN Secretariat is headed by the *Secretary-General*, appointed by the General Assembly, on the recommendation of the Security Council.

The *International Court of Justice* sits in the Hague and consists of 15 judges elected for nine years, with no nation appointing more than one judge at any one time. Its purpose is to hear cases referred to it by member nations and to adjudicate in disputes between nations. Since some countries have said that they will not regard themselves as bound by its decisions (including China, France, Germany and the USA), its real effectiveness is questionable.

World Health Organisation

The *World Health Organisation* is based in Geneva and its work is overseen by the *World Health Assembly* on which all 190 members states are represented. Its work is concerned with providing technical advice and training and implementing programmes in countries on such issues as disease and population control and nutrition.

The Group of Seven (G7)

The Group of Seven leading industrialised countries (known as G7) was established in 1975 to discuss purely economic issues. The organisation is an informal one and has no secretariat. Over the years this informality has led to its discussions broadening to cover political as well as economic issues – such as international terrorism and crime.

The members of G7 are Canada, France, Germany, Italy, Japan, the UK and the USA. There is an Annual Summit of heads of government and the Presidency rotates round the member states.

The informality of the organisation has enabled Russia to take part in the political discussions since 1994.

Other international financial organisations

To complete the international economic picture on an even broader scale, mention should be made of the International Monetary Fund, the World Bank and the Organisation for Economic Co-operation and Development.

The *International Monetary Fund* (IMF) was set up in 1946 and has its headquarters in Washington DC. Its 179 member nations each have a representative on the IMF Board of Governors which meets annually. The IMF exists to administer a code of conduct on exchange rate policies; to provide a source of credit for member countries who are facing problems with their balance of payments; and to provide a forum where member states can discuss international monetary problems.

The *International Bank for Reconstruction and Development* (the *World Bank*), which also has its headquarters in Washington DC, was founded in 1944. The Bank is the source of loans to UN member states to finance economic and social projects in developing countries, although the main thrust of its operations immediately after the Second World War was the reconstruction of Europe.

The *Organisation for Economic Co-operation and Development* (OECD) consists of 25 industrialised countries (including the UK), and is intended to promote economic growth generally, support less developed countries in particular, and promote the expansion of trade throughout the world.

NATO and the Western European Union

The *North Atlantic Treaty Organisation* (NATO) was founded in 1949 in the aftermath of the Second World War and following the emergence of the post-War communist states in the Warsaw Pact. Its *raison d'être* is the collective security of its member states, by deterring aggression, by defending member states against any aggression and by providing a forum for trans-Atlantic allied consultation. In other words, it is a military, rather than a political, organisation.

NATO is important to the UK because the UK's membership of NATO provides the foundation for its defence. Much of the UK's armed forces are committed to NATO.

At the beginning of 1997, there were 16 states in membership of NATO: Belgium, Canada, Denmark, France, Germany, Greece, Iceland, Italy, Luxembourg, the Netherlands, Norway, Portugal, Spain, Turkey, the UK and the USA. Each has a permanent representative in Brussels at the NATO headquarters there. Although a member of NATO, France is not part of the NATO military command structure because President de Gaul pulled France out of that structure in 1966 and it has been slow to rejoin.

The *North Atlantic Council* is the main decision-making body and meets at least twice annually at foreign minister level. The permanent representatives meet weekly. There are many NATO committees at which detailed internal arrangements are discussed.

The NATO military command structure is headed by a *Military Committee* (on which the member countries' Chiefs of Staff sit) under the direction of the North Atlantic Council. Under the Military Committee the command structure divides into: Allied Command Europe, Allied Command Atlantic, Allied Command Channel, Regional Planning Group (for North America) – each with their respective Supreme Commanders. The forces available to NATO fall into three categories: immediate and rapid reaction, main defence and augmentation forces.

Given the basis for the existence of NATO, the highly political issue likely to continue over the next few years is the extent to which membership of NATO itself will be extended to the Baltic and Central European states, most of which were part of the former USSR or the Warsaw Pact, but who now want to join NATO. In May 1997, NATO signed an Accord with Russia, which reassured its concerns over the expansion of NATO in that direction.

In July 1997, the NATO Summit in Madrid agreed, after significant internal dispute, the admission of Poland, Hungary and the Czech Republic – to become full members by 1999; some NATO members would have liked Romania and Slovenia included as well, this time around. The next membership review is due to take place at the next NATO Summit in 1999, coinciding with the 50th anniversary of the foundation of NATO. The 1979 Summit issued an 'open door' statement, making it clear that other states could be invited to join later, provided that they made the right kind of progress.

The problem with admitting former Warsaw Pact and, even more so, the Baltic States, is that their armed forces are, from a purely military point of view, relatively incompetent as individual forces without the central direction and support of the former USSR (and thus of little real immediate value to NATO). Their bases are in the wrong place for their new rôle within NATO. The cost of bringing their forces up to NATO standard will be a considerable burden on the other NATO members or on the new entrants' emerging market-based economies.

NATO's European members form the *Western European Union*, which is a forum for consultation and co-operation on defence issues. Of the European countries in membership of NATO mentioned earlier, Iceland, Norway and Turkey are 'associate members'. Austria, Denmark, Finland, the Irish Republic and Sweden have 'observer' status. – A new class of membership, 'associate partnership', has recently been created and accorded to ten Central European and Baltic states.

The Organisation for Security and Co-operation in Europe (OSCE)

The OSCE now has 54 members. The organisation was set up following the 1975 *Helsinki Final Act* and is intended to promote co-operation between member states on security, human rights and economic matters. The original Helsinki commitments are reviewed at further conferences at regular intervals. In 1990, the states which signed the *Charter of Paris* committed themselves to democracy, human rights and market economies.

Every state in Europe, the states of the former USSR, Canada and the USA are members. The former federal republic of Yugoslavia was suspended from membership in 1992.

The *Permanent Council*, supported by a Secretariat meets in Vienna and takes decisions by consensus. There is an OSCE *High Commissioner on National Minorities*. The officials meet twice each year at conferences organised by the OSCE office in Prague. Advice on democracy, human rights and law is provided by the OSCE *Office for Democratic Institutions and Human Rights*, based in Warsaw.

UK defence strategy

The UK's defence strategy has three broad objectives:

- to deter any threats to and, if necessary, defend the freedom and territorial integrity of the UK and its Dependent Territories, including assistance to the civil authority in countering terrorism;

- to contribute to the promotion of the UK's wider security interests, including the protection of freedom, democratic institutions and free trade; and

- to promote peace and help maximise the international prestige and influence of the UK.

The *UK Dependent Territories* (following the return of Hong Kong to China in July 1997) are the Falkland Islands (subject to a territorial claim by Argentina), Gibraltar (subject to a territorial claim by Spain), the Caribbean Dependent Territories and a range of small islands elsewhere.

The UK defence strategy is implemented by its three armed forces, listed in the order of their creation – the Royal Navy, the British Army and the Royal Air Force.

The UK has its own independent nuclear deterrent which is said to "provide the ultimate guarantee of national security". The present form of that deterrent is two Vanguard class nuclear ballistic missile submarines, built in the UK, carrying US Trident missiles with UK nuclear warheads. A third such submarine is due to enter service in 1998 and a fourth is planned for the turn of the century. With four submarines it should be possible to keep up a permanent patrol at sea while some of the submarines are in for service – presumably, with only two at present this is difficult.

The other form of nuclear deterrent is free-fall air bomb. With the collapse of the former USSR and the apparent end of the Cold War, these bombs are planned for phasing-out by the end of 1998 – leaving Trident as the sole deterrent.

The Ministry of Defence

The Ministry of Defence (MoD) has two rôles – a Department of State (headed by the Secretary of State for Defence) and the highest military HQ of the UK armed forces.

Each armed service has its own *Chief of Staff* who is responsible for the fighting effectiveness, efficiency and morale of that particular service. That responsibility is co-ordinated through the *Chief of the Defence Staff* and the Secretary of State for Defence.

The *Defence Council* which runs the armed forces, is chaired by the Secretary of State. The Council consists of the Chief of the Defence Staff, various Chiefs of Staff and the more senior officers and the civilian officials heading the main departments of the MoD.

Support services are provided by the *Procurement Executive*, the *Defence Intelligence Service*, the *Defence Estates Organisation* and the *Defence Exports Services Organisation*.

The Defence Budget for 1996-97 was £21,425 million. The *Defence Costs Study* has examined all aspects of MoD activity, except the front-line, with a view to achieving greater value for money and clearer direction and accountability. As a consequence, the Defence Budget is expected to fall in real terms over the next few years.

The 1997 New Labour Government

Office titles – Cabinet membership – salaries

● The Prime Minister * (1)

Environment and Transport
● Deputy Prime Minister, Secretary of State for the Environment, Transport and the regions * (2)
● Minister of Transport * (2)
● Environment Minister of State (3)
● Two Ministers of State (3)
● Four Ministers (4)

Treasury
● Chancellor of the Exchequer * (2)
● Chief Secretary to the Treasury * (2)
● Paymaster-General (3)
● Treasury Financial Secretary (3)
● Treasury Economic Secretary (3)

Foreign Office
● Foreign Secretary * (2)
● Foreign and Commonwealth Affairs Minister of State (3)
● Two Ministers of State (3)
● One Minister (4)

International Development §
● Secretary of State for International Development *§ (2)
● One Minister (4)

The Lord Chancellor
- Lord Chancellor * (5)
- Parliamentary Secretary (4)

Law Officers
- Attorney General (6)
- Lord-Advocate (Scotland) (7)
- Solicitor-General (8)
- Solicitor-General for Scotland (9)

Home Office
- Home Secretary * (2)
- Two Ministers of State (3)
- Three Ministers (4)

Education and Employment
- Education and Employment Secretary * (2)
- Three Ministers of State (3)
- Three Ministers (4)

Board of Trade/DTI
- President of the Board of Trade * (2)
- Minister for Trade and Competitiveness in Europe (3)
- Three Ministers of State (3)
- Industry Minister (4)
- One Minister (4)

Agriculture
- Minister of Agriculture, Fisheries and Food * (2)
- One Minister of State (3)
- Two Ministers (4)

Scottish Office
- Scottish Secretary * (2)
- Two Ministers of State (3)
- Three Ministers (4)

Defence
- Defence Secretary * (2)
- Two Ministers of State (3)
- One Minister (4)

Health
- Health Secretary * (2)
- Three Ministers of State (3)
- One Minister (4)

Cabinet Office
- President of the Council and Leader of the House of Commons * (2)
- Lord Privy Seal and Leader of the House of Lords * (10)
- Chancellor of the Duchy of Lancaster * (2)
- Minister without Portfolio (3)
- Parliamentary Under-Secretary (4)

Heritage §§
- National Heritage Secretary * (2)
- One Minister of State (3)
- Two Ministers (4)

Social Security
- Social Security Secretary * (2)
- One Minister of State (3)
- Three Ministers (4)

Northern Ireland
- Northern Ireland Secretary * (2)
- Two Ministers of State (3)
- Minister in the Lords (4)
- One Minister (4)

Wales
- Welsh Secretary * (2)
- Two Ministers (4)

Whips' Office
House of Commons
- Chief Whip (11)
- Deputy Chief Whip (3)
- Two Government Whips (4)
- Five Lord Commissioners of HM Treasury
- Seven Assistant Government Whips

House of Lords
- Captain of the Gentlemen at Arms (Chief Whip)
- Captain of the Yeomen of the Guard (Deputy Chief Whip)
- Five Lords in Waiting (Whips)

Notes
Member of the Cabinet
§ *Overseas Development Administration has been upgraded to Departmental status*
§§ *National Heritage has been renamed: Culture, Media and Sport*

(n) Salaries are: *(1) £100,000*
                        (2) £60,000
                        (3) £31,125
                        (4) £23,623
                        (5) £135,406
                        (6) £63,756
                        (7) £78,072
                        (8) £78,042
                        (9) £66,811
                        (10) £77,963
                        (11) £36,613

– The salaries quoted are in addition to the basic MP salary of £43,860, except for those in the Lords.
– The Prime Minister has said that he will not draw his full salary.
– The Minister for Trade and Competitiveness in Europe has declined to draw his ministerial salary.

Government Departments and Agencies

Departments and their more important Agencies as at 1997 listed by area of activity

[Agencies are in *italics* and Cabinet Ministries are marked *; § see note at end].

The Cabinet Office (Office of Public Service)
- The Buying Agency
- Central Computer and Telecommunications Agency
- Civil Service College
- Occupational Health and Safety Agency
- Central Office of Information (reports to the Chancellor of the Duchy of Lancaster)

ECONOMIC AFFAIRS

Ministry of Agriculture, Fisheries and Food *
- Central Science Laboratory
- Intervention Board
- Meat Hygiene Service
- Pesticides Safety Directorate
- Laboratories Agency
- Veterinary Medicine Directorate

Department of Trade and Industry *
- Companies House
- Insolvency Service
- Patent Office

Department of Transport * §
- Coastguard Agency
- Driver and Vehicle Licensing Agency
- Driving Standards Agency
- Highways Agency
- Marine Safety Agency
- Transport Research Laboratory
- Vehicle Inspectorate

HM Treasury *
HM Customs and Excise
Export Credits Guarantee Department (ECGD)
Inland Revenue
- Valuation Office

Executive Agencies overseen by a Minister of State within HM Treasury:
- Royal Mint
- The Office of HM Paymaster General
- Office for National Statistics

REGULATORY BODIES

Office of Electricity Regulation (OFFER)
Office of Gas Supply (OFGAS)
Office of the National Lottery (OFLOT)
Office of Passenger Rail Franchise (OPRAF)
Office for Standards in Education (OFSTED)
Office of Telecommunications (OFTEL)
Office of Water Services (OFWAT)

LEGAL AFFAIRS

Lord Chancellor's Department *
- The Court Service
- HM Land Registry
- Public Record Office
- Public Trust Office

Crown Prosecution Service
Legal Secretariat to the Law Officers
Parliamentary Counsel
HM Procurator General and Treasury Solicitor
- Government Property Lawyers
- The Treasury Solicitor's Department

Lord Advocate's Department and Crown Office
Serious Fraud Office

EXTERNAL AFFAIRS AND DEFENCE

Ministry of Defence *
- Hydrographic Office
- Meteorological Office
- Ministry of Defence Police

Foreign and Commonwealth Office *

International Development *
- Natural Resources Institute

SOCIAL AFFAIRS, THE ENVIRONMENT AND CULTURE

Department for Education and Employment *
- Employment Service
- Teachers' Pensions Agency

Department of the Environment * §
- Building Research Establishment
- Planning Inspectorate
- Queen Elizabeth II Conference Centre

Department of Health *
- Medicines Control Agency
- NHS Estates
- NHS Pensions Agency

Home Office *
- Fire Service College
- Forensic Science Service
- HM Prison Service
- UK Passport Agency

Department of Culture, Media and Sport *
- Historic Royal Palaces Agency
- Royal Parks Agency

Department of Social Security *
- Benefits Agency
- Child Support Agency
- Contributions Agency
- War Pensions Agency

OTHERS

Her Majesty's Stationery Office (HMSO)
Ordnance Survey (OS)
Office of the Data Protection Registrar

THE NORTHERN IRELAND OFFICE *

Department of Agriculture for Northern Ireland
Department of Economic Development for Northern Ireland
Department of Education for Northern Ireland
Department of the Environment for Northern Ireland
Department of Finance and Personnel
Department of Health and Social Services for Northern Ireland

THE SCOTTISH OFFICE *

Scottish Office Agriculture, Environment and Fisheries Department
Scottish Office Development Department
Scottish Office Education and Industry Department
Scottish Office Department of Health
Scottish Office Home Department and Courts Administration
Lord Advocate's Department
Crown Office

THE WELSH OFFICE *

Note: At various times in the past, the Department of the Environment and the Department of Transport have worked together on a semi-integrated basis, especially at regional level. The New Labour Government, shortly after it came into office, announced its intention to merge the two Departments into a new Superministry: the Department of the Environment, Transport and the Regions *– to reflect the departmental rôle of the Deputy Prime Minister, John Prescott (described by* The Guardian *as the "Minister for Everything").*

APPENDIX C

Useful Information Sources

Advisory, Conciliation and Arbitration Service (ACAS)
27 Wilton Street, London SWIX 7AZ
Tel: 0171 210 3000

Ministry of Agriculture, Fisheries and Food (MAFF)
3-8 Whitehall Place, London SWIA 2HH
Tel: 0171 270 3000

Arts Council of Great Britain
14 Great Peter Street, London SWIP 3NQ
Tel: 0171 333 0100

British Council
10 Spring Gardens, London SWIA 2BN
Tel: 0171 930 8466

British Waterways Board
Willow Grange, Church Road, Watford, Herts., WDI 3QA
Tel: 01923 226422

Buckingham Palace Press Office
Buckingham Palace, London SWIA IAA
Tel: 0171 930 4832

Cabinet Office (Office of Public Service)
70 Whitehall, London SWIA 2AS
Tel: 0171 270 1234

Charity Commission
St Albans House, 57/60 Haymarket, London SWIY 4QX
Tel: 0171 210 4477

Civil Aviation Authority (CAA)
CAA House, 45-59 Kingsway, London WC2B 6TE
Tel: 0171 379 7311

Citizen's Charter Unit
Cabinet Office, Government Offices,
Great George Street, London SWIA 2AS
Tel: 0171 270 1826

Confederation of British Industry (CBI)
Centre Point, 103 New Oxford Street, London WCIA IDU
Tel: 0171 379 7400

Crown Prosecution Service (CPS)
50 Ludgate Hill, London EC4M 7EX
Tel: 0171 273 8000

H.M. Customs and Excise
New King's Beam House, 22 Upper Ground, London SEI 9PJ
Tel: 0171 620 1313

Office of the Data Protection Registrar
Wycliffe House, Water Lane, Wilmslow, SK9 5AF
Tel: 01625 545745

Ministry of Defence
Main Building, Whitehall, London SWIA 2HB
Tel: 0171 218 9000

Department of Education and Employment (DfEE)
Sanctuary Buildings, Great Smith Street, London SWIP 3BT
Tel: 0171 925 5000

Department of the Environment (DoE)
2 Marsham Street, London SWIP 3EB
Tel: 0171 276 0900

European Communities, Commission of the UK (Office)
8 Storey's Gate, London SWIP 3AT
Tel: 0171 973 1992

European Parliament Information Office
2 Queen Anne's Gate, London SWIH 9AA
Tel: 0171 222 0411

Office of Fair Trading (OFT)
Field House, Breams Buildings, London EC4A IPR
Tel: 0171 242 2858

Foreign and Commonwealth Office
Downing Street, London SWIA 2AL.
Tel: 0171 270 1500

Health and Safety Commission (HSC)
Rose Court, 2 Southwark Bridge, London SEI 9HE
Tel: 0171 717 6000

Department of Health (DoH)
Richmond House, 79 Whitehall, London SWIA 2NS
Tel: 0171 210 3000

Health Service Commissioner (Ombudsman)
Church House, Great Smith Street, London SWIP 3BW
Tel: 0171 276 2035

Her Majesty's Stationery Office (HMSO)
St Clements House, 2-16 Colegate, Norwich NR3 1BQ
Tel: 01603 621000

Home Office
Queen Anne's Gate, London SWI 9AT
Tel: 0171 273 3000

House of Commons
London SWIA OAA
Tel: 0171 219 3000

House of Lords
London SWIA OPW
Tel: 0171 219 3000

Central Office of Information
Hercules Road, London SEI 7DU
Tel: 0171 928 2345

Inland Revenue
Somerset House, London WC2R 1LB
Tel: 0171 438 6622

Lord Chancellor's Department
Selborne House, 54-60 Victoria Street, London SW1E 6QW
Tel: 0171 210 8500

Metropolitan Police
New Scotland Yard, Broadway, London SWIH OBG
Tel: 0171 230 1212

Department of National Heritage (DNH)
2-4 Cockspur Street, London SWIY 5DH
Tel: 0171 211 6000

Office for National Statistics
Great George Street, London SW1P 3AQ
Tel 0171 270 3000

Nature Conservancy Council (English Nature)
Northminster House, Peterborough PEI IUA
Tel: 01733 340345

Northern Ireland Office
Stormont Castle, Belfast BT4 3ST
Tel: 01232 520700
Whitehall, London SW1A 2AZ
Tel: 0171 210 3000

Office of Electricity Regulation (OFFER)
Hagley House, Hagley Road, Birmingham B16 8QG
Tel: 0121 456 2100

Office of Gas Supply (OFGAS)
Stockley House, 130 Wilton Road, London SW1V 1LQ
Tel: 0171 828 0898

Office of the National Lottery (OFLOT)
2 Monck Street, London SW1P 2BQ
Tel: 0171 227 2000

Office for Standards in Education (OFSTED)
29-33 Kingsway, London WC2B 6SE
Tel: 0171 925 6800

Office of Telecommunications (OFTEL)
50 Ludgate Hill, London EC4M 7JJ
Tel 0171 634 8700

Office of Water Services (OFWAT)
Centre City Tower, 7 Hill Street, Birmingham B5 4UA
Tel: 0121 625 1300

Ordnance Survey (OS)
Romsey Road, Southampton SO16 4GU
Tel: 01703 792000

Overseas Development Administration (ODA)
94 Victoria Street, London SW1E 5JL
Tel: 0171 917 7000

Parliamentary Commissioner for Administration (Ombudsman)
Church House, Great Smith Street, London SWIP 3BW
Tel: 0171 276 2130

Office of H.M. Paymaster General
Sutherland House, Russell Way, Crawley, RH10 1UH
Tel: 01293 560999

Police Complaints Authority
10 Great George Street, London SWIP 3AE
Tel: 0171 273 6450

The Post Office
5th Floor, 148 Old Street, London ECIV 9HQ
Tel: 0171 490 2888

Prime Minister's Office
10 Downing Street, London SWIA 2AA
Tel: 0171 270 3000

Royal Mint
Llantrisant, Pontyclun, Mid Glamorgan CF72 8YT
Tel: 01443 222111

The Scottish Office
St Andrew's House, Edinburgh EH1 3TG
Tel: 0131 556 8400
Dover House, Whitehall, London SW1A 2AU
Tel: 0171 270 3000

Department of Social Security (DSS)
Richmond House, 79 Whitehall, London SWIA 2NS
Tel: 0171 210 3000

Sports Council
16 Upper Woburn Place, London WCIH OQP
Tel: 0171 388 1277

Department of Trade and Industry (DTI)
123 Victoria Street, London SWIE 6RB
Tel: 0171 215 5000

Trades Union Congress (TUC)
Congress House, Great Russell Street, London WCIB 3LS
Tel: 0171 636 4030

Department of Transport (DoT)
Great Minster House, 76 Marsham Street, London SWIP 4DR
Tel: 0171 271 5000

H.M. Treasury
Information Division, Treasury Chambers,
Parliament Street, London SWIP 3AG
Tel: 0171 270 3000

Welsh Office
Cathays Park, Cardiff CFI 3NQ
Tel: 01222 825111
Gwydyr House, Whitehall, London SW1A 2ER
Tel: 0171 270 3000

Additional telephone numbers for government departments and public corporations can be found in the Central Office of Information pamphlet:
Information, Press and Public Relations Officers

OTHER USEFUL REFERENCE SOURCES

– *Britain [1997]: An Official Handbook (HMSO) – published annually*
– *Dodds — Parliamentary Companion*
– *Vacher's Parliamentary Companion*
– *Whitakers Almanac*

BRITISH COMPANIES INFORMATION SOURCES

There is a number of useful sources which journalists may use to find information on companies:

- *Companies Registration Office Directory* (Companies House, Cardiff): All companies have by law to register and this register lists some 850,000 companies with their registered address, date of establishment and date of latest annual returns. Information is available by post;

- *Kelly's Manufacturers and Merchants Directory* (75,000 entries);

- *Sell's Directory of Products and Services* (60,000 entries);

- *Kompass Register of British Industry and Commerce* (30,000 entries);

- *Key British Enterprises* (20,000 entries).

Index